MAKING A BALLET

Making a ballet takes an unbounded patience from everybody concerned. An outsider is fascinated to be let in on the minuteness of the workmanship. But then he finds no way out of that minuteness. Listening to the same few bars pounded again and again on the piano, watching the same movements started at top speed and broken off, again and again, the fascinated outsider after two hours and a half of that finds himself going stir crazy. Seeing a ballet in the theatre the momentum of action and music carries the audience into a world of zest and grandeur. In performance the dancers look ravishing. In rehearsal they look like exhausted champions attempting Mt. Everest, knowing how limited the time is, step by step, hold by hold, roped together by the music, with the peak nowhere in sight.

Edwin Denby, *Dancers, Buildings and People in the Streets*, Horizon Press, New York, 1965.

MARY CLARKE
AND
CLEMENT CRISP

Making a Ballet

The Choreographer Speaks

faber and faber

This edition first published in 2010
by Faber and Faber Ltd
Bloomsbury House, 74–77 Great Russell Street
London WC1B 3DA

Printed by CPI Antony Rowe, Eastbourne

A CIP record for this book is available from the British Library

ISBN 978–0–571–25963–2

CONTENTS

We dedicate this book to

Marian Eames with our gratitude for her work on *Dance Index* and for the pleasure of her company in New York and London; to Lincoln Kirstein as a small thank you for his immense achievement; and to Andrew Porter, critic and friend. It is for all of them as a souvenir of hilarious dinner parties in Brompton Square.

ACKNOWLEDGEMENTS

This book would not have been possible were it not for the kindness and generosity of a great many creative artists. We started under the happy auspices of a conversation with Paul Taylor during his London season in 1973, when he talked most illuminatingly about his work; his testimony can be found throughout the book. Each one of our generous 'collaborators' found time in the middle of their creativity to talk to us, and we should here point out that all their comments come from tape recordings and are transcribed as direct speech rather than as polished and considered written testimony.

Richard Alston talked just after completing a ballet; David Blair talked in the summer which followed his farewell as a dancer in his most famous role of Colas in *La Fille mal Gardée*; Christopher Bruce took time from a rehearsal; Elizabeth Dalton not only talked but fed us chocolate cake; Peter Darrell gave up precious time from directing and choreographing; Kenneth MacMillan snatched an afternoon from his many responsibilities as director of the Royal Ballet; Barry Moreland was embarking on a new ballet; Norman Morrice had finished a work for his company's triumphant return to Sadler's Wells Theatre; Thea Musgrave and her husband Peter Mark were on a flying visit to London; Kenneth Rowell was about to leave for Australia and was also working on the Australian Ballet's London season; Lynn Seymour gave generously of her time in between rehearsals; and Glen Tetley, paying a brief visit to London, was also most kind. Both Valerie Bourne of the Ballet Rambert and Margaret Sedwards of Sadler's Wells Theatre were enormously helpful in arranging interviews for us. Carol Venn was, as ever, exemplary in handling our manuscript, and Mme Sackova lent her customary encouragement and support.

Special thanks are due to Joan Lawson for permission to reproduce her invaluable transcriptions of Petipa's notes on *The Sleeping Beauty* and *The Nutcracker*; to Ivor Guest and John Lanchbery for permission to use the article on the music of *La Fille mal Gardée*; to Natalia Roslavleva for allowing us to reprint her article on *How a Soviet Ballet is Made*; to Tatiana Loguine for permission to use the translation of Nijinska's article about *Les Noces*; to Peter Williams for permission to quote from *Dance and Dancers*; to Selma Jeanne Cohen for permission to quote from *Dance Perspectives*; to Nicholas Johnson for posing for illustrations, and to Anthony Crickmay for taking them.

Introduction

The techniques of writing a play, composing an opera, even making a film, are comparatively well known and understood by the general public, but it has seemed to us that the extraordinarily complex procedures that go to make up a ballet are still wrapt in mystery. Dancing is the most difficult of arts to explain; its techniques are remote from popular understanding; its vocabulary is still described in a foreign language. The dancer's life is led in an almost secret world of daily practice in the classroom and incessant rehearsal. Dancers are more clannish than even musicians or actors. We should like to clear away some of the misconceptions – typified by the lady who watched a ballet and said, 'I don't know how they manage to make it up so cleverly as they go along' – and the mystique that surrounds what is, after all, a hard-learned and very arduous craft no more mysterious than cabinet-making. The great choreographer George Balanchine has described himself not only as a cabinet-maker, but also as a cook.

We have mentioned the dancer first because the dancer is the basic material, but it is the choreographer who builds the balletic structure from the dancers' bodies and their training, using the musical score as a foundation for his work, and calling upon the designer to provide decoration and setting. This is still the usual form of collaboration, one that has been perfected over the past two centuries, but it is not a rigid formula and indeed the post-World War II years have brought remarkable and fascinating changes which we shall also discuss.

The classic academic ballet technique is one of the highest forms of human physical activity and its development and adaptation will be one of the constant themes of this book. It is, however, also a jumping-off ground for many other forms of movement. Modern dance was a reaction against it, and of recent years there has been a quite remarkable cross-fertilization between these two disciplines and the new approach to both classic ballet and modern dance has provided the impulse for new choreography and for new thinking about the function of dance in the theatre and in society.

The classic technique, which had been codified by the beginning of the nineteenth century, has developed enormously since then, and is still developing. Dancers today are different in physique – leaner, faster, taller – their training is infinitely more scientific and wider in range (though the basic truths are still respected in the daily class). The medical profession has become involved not only in the treatment of injuries but also in their prevention and in the supervision of the actual physical development of dancers. Choreographers ask for new things from dancers; the skills required are mastered in the schools; conversely, new skills offer new challenges to the choreographers.

To appreciate the current state of ballet-making, it is important to understand the nineteenth-century background from which it has sprung. Our first chapter, accordingly, will deal with the heritage that is the common ground from which most of today's choreography springs.

In Denmark and Russia, the direct descendants of nineteenth-century dancers and choreographers still delight in preserving their great inheritance. New national companies – Britain's Royal Ballet is the supreme example – have been given the soundest of foundations by the acquisition of a body of nine-teenth-century classics.

Some of the bravest and most fruitful experiments of the Diaghilev Ballet are preserved throughout the world, as an example and an inspiration. This inheritance is the point of departure for a great deal of what is happening today. In this book we hope to show the relevance of the changes in conditions of work and methods of collaboration between choreographer, designers, composer and dancer.

Finally, and most important, we hope through direct testimony of creators to give an insight to today's audience of how a ballet is made.

The inheritance

It is convenient and usual to date the form of ballet as we know it today from the time of the Romantic movement in France. The massive social, political and industrial upheavals that resulted from the Napoleonic wars, the Industrial Revolution and the destruction of the old Europe of the *ancien régime* inevitably produced a need to reassess and rethink the arts.

The neo-classic movement at the beginning of the nineteenth century gave way to the richer emotional attitudes of Romanticism by the 1830s. Such creators as Berlioz, Géricault, Victor Hugo, Lamartine are symptomatic of this change. Eighteenth-century ballet had been concerned with the heroic and mythological aspects of classicism. A dance technique had evolved of some considerable brilliance which persisted into the nineteenth century and formed and still forms the basis of the academic dance. In the teaching and writings of the Italian ballet master Carlo Blasis – *The Code of Terpsichore*, 1828 and *The Elementary Treatise*, 1820 – we can see a vocabulary no different in its rules from that practised today. But Romanticism gave it a different flavour and a different impulse. The domination of the male dancer in the eighteenth century – exemplified by Gaëtan Vestris and his son Auguste – was to yield to the supremacy of the Romantic ballerinas such as Taglioni and Elssler. Their technique, though, was still that of Vestris, who was one of the teachers of Elssler.

The crucial breakthrough came with the arrival in Paris of Marie Taglioni in 1827. Formed by the rigorous training of her father Filippo Taglioni, who decided to capitalize on her physical gifts of lightness, grace and demure charm, Marie Taglioni became the precise image of the new Romantic dancer, and *La Sylphide*, 1832, revealed it to an astonished and delighted world. It is worth noting that this image persists even today both in the silhouette of the female dancer (the sleek hair, the long floating tarlatans), and in the desire for aerial grace, which is the goal for every ballerina. Fanny Elssler was the other side of the Romantic coin. Voluptuous, brilliant, dramatically exciting, she was the pagan dancer (as Gautier called her) opposed to the 'Christian' art of Taglioni. Both of these artists and their contemporaries illustrate the merits and also the inherent sterility of Romanticism: the ballerina had become either an un-attainable ideal (the Sylphide or Giselle) or the all-too-attainable seductress.

It was in Copenhagen that Romanticism found a lasting and fruitful develop-ment thanks to the creativity of August Bournonville. Bournonville accepted and enhanced the eighteenth-century technique which he acquired from his years of training with Auguste Vestris in Paris. He worshipped Taglioni, partnered her, and called her his ideal but he could not subscribe to the female domination of the Romantic ballerina seen in Paris and London. Bournonville was too good a dancer and too good a choreographer to wish to perpetuate the

NOTICE SUR LA SYLPHIDE

Un jour, poussé par la fantaisie, la seule muse qui l'ait trouvé docile, notre ami Charles Nodier s'en va visiter les montagnes de l'Écosse. Charmant voyage d'un bel esprit oisif et rêveur, qui s'inquiète fort peu de savoir ce que va dire la *Revue d'Édimbourg*! Pâle et douce image d'un poète insouciant qui croit avoir tout fait pour la gloire et surtout pour la joie intérieure, quand d'une course aux pays lointains il rapporte moins que rien, un conte, un rêve, une ballade. — Nodier, en effet, rapportait de son voyage en Écosse l'histoire de Trilby : Trilby, c'est le bon génie du foyer domestique, c'est le diable amoureux qui

GISELLE

Giselle est le premier ballet que Carlotta Grisi ait dansé à l'Opéra, où elle avait débuté par ce pas si brillant de *la Favorite*, qui est encore un des plus beaux fleurons de sa couronne chorégraphique. On se souvenait bien d'avoir vu, il y a quelques années, à la Renaissance, une charmante enfant qui jouait un rôle dans une pièce intitulée *Zingaro*; mais l'on ne savait pas si c'était une danseuse ou une chanteuse, car elle était l'une et l'autre. Une voix fraîche, pure et juste, une danse légère et correcte, de beaux yeux bleus d'une douce naïveté, voilà ce que Carlotta Grisi avait laissé dans la mémoire des gens du monde et des feuilletonistes. *Giselle* la plaça tout d'un coup au premier rang. Un poète de nos amis trouva dans une légende allemande, pour cette blonde

rejection of the male dancer that obtained in the great centres of dancing in the West. In what was in fact an artistic backwater Bournonville guided the Royal Danish Ballet in Copenhagen for nearly fifty years, producing a remarkable series of ballets that reflected a concern for dramatic truth, poetically evoked the scenes he knew from his travels in Spain and Italy, from his feeling for Danish history, and demonstrated his clear belief that dancing was a joyous and ennobling activity worthy of the participation of the most serious and gifted members of society.

In another remote centre, Imperial Petersburg, the Romantic dance flourished and it is not an exaggeration to say that ballet was preserved there. Russian ballet in the eighteenth and nineteenth centuries owed everything to the participation of foreign choreographers and teachers. Richly endowed by the Tsar, whose servants the artists of the ballet were, the Imperial Ballet existed to entertain the Court that surrounded this absolute monarch. First Charles Didelot, then Jules Perrot, then Arthur St Léon – all French ballet masters – had been responsible for the repertory in Petersburg, but it was the activities of Marius Petipa that were to be of the greatest influence. Engaged as a principal dancer in 1847, Petipa had to wait until 1869 to achieve his aim of becoming first ballet master to the Imperial Ballet. Over a period of forty years, from 1862 to 1903, he produced a series of *ballets à grand spectacle* to enshrine the massive forces and ever developing technical skill of the Russian dancers. Often leading rôles were taken by guest artists, usually Italian virtuoso ballerinas, products of the Milanese school of Carlo Blasis which offered the most brilliant training

Left Engraving from *Les Beautés de l'Opéra* published in Paris in 1845, showing the opening pose of *La Sylphide* with Taglioni kneeling beside the sleeping James (Mazilier)

Right Carlotta Grisi and Lucien Petipa in the opening scene of *Giselle* from *Les Beautés de l'Opéra*

Above The Royal Danish Ballet in the current production of Bournonville's *Napoli*. Niels Bjorn Larsen and Fredbjorn Bjornsson as the two comic mimes

Right The Royal Danish Ballet in Bournonville's *Konservatoriet* as performed today

of the time; and their participation was important for the inspiration it offered to the development of technique in Russia.

Petipa's procedure in creating his big ballets – three- and four-act spectacles which lasted a whole evening and were designed to titillate the taste of his Court audience – seems to have been codified early on. Having chosen his theme, which in many cases would have been suggested by contemporary events, he drafted a very clear libretto breaking up the action into scenes and actual numbers, and it is from this detailed libretto that he started work. The writing of the score was entrusted to that remarkable figure the 'official' composer of ballet music to the theatre – two incumbents of the position during Petipa's time were Pugni and Minkus – and they were required to furnish precisely measured numbers: processions, ballabili, polkas, waltzes, variations, pas de deux, whose dramatic point was rarely considered in the writing. The scores thus stitched together were not inspired, they merely provided the sort of serviceable rum-ti-tum accompaniment to which audiences were accustomed and they made neither the choreographer nor the dancers think at all. Of dramatic sense, reason, verisimilitude there was not a trace, and anyone interested in savouring the full idiocy of the plots should read the scenario for *Pharoah's Daughter* to be found in Cyril Beaumont's invaluable *Complete Book of Ballets*.

There was no more sense in the design. Sets were created to rigid formulae: they were provided by the paint shops and official scenic artists to the theatre who could devise temples or palaces or forest scenes with no more thought than went into the creation of the score. Costume followed certain rigid rules: the ballerina must wear pink toe-shoes and a tutu. If the ballet were Egyptian her skirt might have some Egyptian decoration; were it Greek, a border of the key

The death scene from Act III of Petipa's *La Bayadère* as given at the Bolshoy Theatre Petersburg in 1877 with Ekaterina Vazem as the heroine Nikiya. A contemporary engraving

A set for the original production of Petipa's *The Sleeping Beauty* at the Maryinsky Theatre, Petersburg, 1890. From a contemporary photograph

pattern would suffice. Tightly corseted, hung about with her own jewels, partnered respectfully by a premier danseur whose costuming was modest rather than truthful, the ballerina knew that in each act she would have a brilliant variation and a pas de deux, just as the soloists knew that they would have a pas de trois or pas de quatre in which they might show off their virtuosity, while the corps de ballet were on certain occasions required to bring on wooden blocks and pose on top of them to form agreeable but inanimate groupings in front of which the more important members of the cast would go through their tricks.

Despite these rigid conventions, which became more rigid as Petipa's dominion over the ballet continued, those fragments of the ballets which survive prove his great talent – witness the Kingdom of Shades scene from his *La Bayadère* and what remains of his Grand Pas in *Paquita*. He was effortlessly inventive, constantly seeking the expansion of technique and, within his own terms, adventurous. He was reluctant to go on producing the same ballet year after year (this being his instruction from the director of the theatre) but his aristocratic audience was ultra-conservative and even to the very last he was providing the same cumbersome, albeit glittering spectacles. Even when in 1888 he set to work on his masterpiece *The Sleeping Beauty* he furnished the composer with the kind of instructions that he had offered Minkus and Pugni and we can give the best idea of these by referring you to Appendix A.

In her *A History of Ballet and its Makers* Joan Lawson states that Petipa described his recipe for making a ballet as follows:

> He examined each step of the classic vocabulary, assessing its merit and quality as it were, and allotting it to one of the seven categories of movement so that it could:
>
> 1 Be a preparation or provide a link between one movement and the next. (The auxiliary or preparatory steps.)
>
> 2 Add lightness, height, depth and breadth to the dance. (Steps of grande and petite élévation.)
>
> 3 Add brilliance and sparkle, even wit. (Grande and petite batterie.)
>
> 4 Lend continuity to the flow of line, help to the movement and complete the total pattern of the steps. (The ports de bras.)
>
> 5 Add speed and excitement. (Pirouettes.)
>
> 6 Become the highlight or finishing point of an enchaînement or dance. (Poses.)
>
> 7 Lend the finishing touch to the total picture. (Pointes which he always used with the greatest discretion and finesse.)

Nicholas Legat, at that time a principal male dancer of the Imperial Ballet, offers an extraordinary description of Petipa at work, revealing both the formal procedures and also the technical and dramatic vitality that the old master could infuse into his creations:

> Whenever Petipa set about producing a ballet he waited till absolute silence reigned in the hall. Then, consulting the notes he had composed at home he would methodically begin work. He worked on many of his groupings at home, where he used little figures like chess pawns to represent dancers, arranging them all over the table. He would spend long hours studying these groupings and write down the successful ones in his notebook. Separate numbers, solos and pas de deux he composed at the rehearsals.
>
> First he had the music played through. Then he would sit for a time in deep thought. Then he would usually ask for the music to be played again, imagining the dance, making little gestures, and moving his eyebrows. In the middle he would jump up and cry 'Enough'. He would then compose the dance eight bars at a time, call the dancer to him, and explain the movements at first in words rather than gestures. The whole dance having been explained, the dancer began again from the beginning, while Petipa frequently stopped, corrected or modified the movements. In the end he would say: 'Now try nice,' which meant the artiste might try to execute the finished dance.
>
> For women Petipa was the ideal dance composer. He had an amazing capacity for finding the most advantageous movements for each danseuse, so that the end result looked both simple and graceful. He rarely gave combinations involving high technique, but paid chief attention to grace and beauty of line and pose.
>
> For men, he was unable to compose effective dances. We almost always had to modify or develop them to suit our style, and we used to consult Johannson [the great Swedish dancer and teacher who was a pupil of Bournonville, and who settled in Petersburg and both

influenced and enriched the training in the Imperial schools] on this, he being for men what Petipa was for women as a dance composer.

The most fascinating moments of all were those when Petipa composed his mimic scenes. Showing each participant in turn he would get quite carried away by the parts, and the whole hall would sit with bated breath, following the extraordinary expressive mimicry of this artistic giant. When the scene was set there would be a terrific outburst of applause, but Petipa paid little attention. He would return quietly to his seat, smiling and licking his lips in a characteristic gesture, lighting a cigarette, and sitting silent for a time. Then the whole scene would be repeated while Petipa put finishing touches to the actions of the individual artistes. (Nicholas Legat, *The Story of the Russian School*, British Continental Press Ltd, 1932.)

Much of this dramatic colour and mimetic brilliance has been omitted in later stagings of the Petipa repertory, and it is unwise to judge Petipa wholly upon what we see today.

With the turn of the century and the end of Petipa's long reign, a reaction was inevitable though this did not take the form that might have been envisaged. Petipa left no heirs to continue the tradition of the long ballet. The form itself was moribund and with his retirement in 1903 the Imperial Ballet sank into a period of creative inanition from which it was only to be roused, like Russia itself, by the Revolution. The new ballet, though, was to come from Russia, spearheaded by the new thinking of a young dancer in the Imperial Ballet, Mikhail Fokine. When he joined the Maryinsky troupe in 1898 Fokine seemed destined for a great career as a male dancer. He soon became profoundly dis-satisfied with the encrusted traditionalism of what he was called upon to dance, a traditionalism that had reduced dramatic expression to the stereotyped language of mime. The attempt made by the Romantic ballet d'action to fuse drama and dance as in *La Sylphide* and *Giselle* had become ponderous and inexpressive as it relied more and more on an almost secret vocabulary of gesture. Odette's mime narrative to Siegfried at the beginning of Act II of *Swan Lake* is artificial and incomprehensible to today's audience ('I am the Queen of the Swans; there is a lake made of my mother's tears; over there is one, a wicked enchanter, who me a swan did make; if one loves me, swears to be true, I no longer a swan shall be' – the prose reflects the order of the mime gestures). Performed in the original dramatic style this language could be used for notable effects: Karsavina revived both the Wili legend narrated by Berthe in *Giselle* and Lise's daydream in the second act of *La Fille mal Gardée* to suggest an emotional vivacity. Potentially enlivening, mime became a symbol of the threadbare and insensitive to Fokine. His creative rejection of it in favour of a truer language in which the whole body 'spoke' showed the way for much of twentieth-century dramatic dancing. A man of wide culture, Fokine was eager to bring greater truth into ballet; by 1904 he had approached the Maryinsky directorate with ideas for a ballet which would exemplify his concern for dramatic truth reflected not only in the steps but also in the design and in the music. It is symptomatic that when he sought to present a Grecian scene in his ballet *Eunice* he was forbidden to bring bare-foot dancers on to the stage of the Maryinsky Theatre and instead, as he notes in his memoirs, 'we painted toes on the feet of tights, even pink toenails and rouge on the knees and heels'. And he was advised 'It is impossible to bring the ballerina out on stage without her tutu, to deny her effective dances in which she can display the brilliance of her technique.'

Fokine's innovation and his desire for a new sort of ballet reflected an unease with traditionalism that was being felt in the other arts and it was inevitable that before long he should encounter Serge Diaghilev. Over the period of a decade, from 1895 to 1905, Diaghilev had established a reputation as an arbiter of artistic taste and one of the chief representatives of the new feeling in the world of painting in particular. With his associates, Alexandre Benois and Léon Bakst, he had edited an influential art magazine, he had been responsible for a series of exceptional exhibitions of painting which had brought Western art into Russia, and had also revealed the glories of Russian art to the fashionable world of Petersburg. By 1906 Diaghilev was concerning himself with showing Russian art to the West. A very successful exhibition of Russian art in Paris had been followed by concerts of Russian music and in 1908 by a season of Russian opera, centred round the great talent of Chaliapine.

It was inevitable that Diaghilev should want to show the glories of the young generation of Russian dancers, the marvellous products of the traditional training that had been perfected under Petipa's régime. But it would be unthinkable to show these dancers in the old-fashioned and cumbersome ballets that were to be seen in Petersburg. Hence it was to Fokine that Diaghilev and Benois turned to provide a repertory to show off artists like Karsavina, Pavlova, Nijinsky and Bolm, for the Paris season of Russian Opera and Ballet in 1909.

Tamara Karsavina, the ballerina who was Fokine's muse and inspiration in the early seasons of the Diaghilev Ballet, has described his method of work:

> Of course, Fokine put in some preparatory work: listening to music, visualizing the movement in its broad outline; but I doubt whether he ever worked at his desk, meticulously filling in the steps bar by bar. His real work began when his plastic material was at hand – his dancers and himself together.
>
> He did not compose from the chair, telling one to do this or that. He himself danced in front of us. It was then that his inspiration took definite shape, the spring of instinctive motion being released.
>
> It is easy to see that in his classical ballets he never deviated from academic tradition except in pruning from it any form of exhibitionism, and in giving it more expression: the more supple unhackneyed movements of arms and a more ingenious ground pattern.
>
> In spite of the total absence of any obvious *tours de force* his classic choreography was more difficult to the interpreter than almost any part in the legitimate repertoire. He would not be satisfied with a merely correct step; to please him the step had to reach up to that ideal which exists in the mind of the producer. (Tamara Karsavina, 'Fokine's two great careers', *Dance and Dancers*, May 1955.)

It was the artistic brilliance of Benois and Bakst that provided the decorative key to the Paris season of 1909. The phenomenon of this first appearance of the Russian Ballet in the West marks an entirely new period in the history of ballet and indeed of stage design and music in the theatre. For the first time we see the artistic collaboration which is the hallmark of modern ballet. Diaghilev was insistent upon the closest possible consultation between the creators of a ballet. He acted as catalyst, arbiter and ultimately as dictator, and his genius must often seem no less than that of the talents he employed – Stravinsky, Bakst, Fokine and that great catalogue of creators who worked for him during the next twenty years.

The supreme example of such collaboration in the years before World War I is to be seen in *Petrushka*. Diaghilev had already discovered Igor Stravinsky and had commissioned from him the score for *The Firebird*, which in Fokine's

choreography had been the triumph of the second Paris season by the Russian dancers in 1910. During the following winter Stravinsky had played to Diaghilev a sort of Russian dance and another piece which he had named 'Petrushka's Cry'. Benois notes: 'They had both had the idea of using this music for some new ballet, but no story had as yet been devised. They had only conceived the idea of representing the Petersburg carnival and including in it a performance of Petrushka the Russian Punch and Judy show. "Who else but you," wrote Diaghilev, "could help us with this problem?"' Within a short time Benois and Stravinsky were planning the work with Diaghilev, meeting daily to discuss the shape of the ballet although the detailed action had not yet been decided. The collaboration continued even when Stravinsky was in Switzerland and Benois in Petersburg, and 'the subject was acquiring definite shape' as were the personalities of the three chief characters. The closing scene was worked on when Stravinsky and Benois met again with Diaghilev in Rome, where the Russian dancers were to appear in 1911, and Fokine started work as soon as the score was completed, labouring under the most appalling conditions in a cellar in Rome and continuing in Paris under equally unfavourable circumstances. He observed:

I joined my collaborators after the main characters of the story and the primary lines of its development had already been created by them. Nevertheless when I say *my* ballet *Petrushka*, when I add that it was one of the most successful and outstanding of *my* compositions, I feel that I am perfectly justified in doing this. One could call it a musico-dramatic composition by Stravinsky ... one could say that it was one of the greatest works of Benois. One could also classify *Petrushka* as a Fokine production which was one of the most complete demonstrations of his application of ballet reforms ... Each one of us, in his own language, told of Petrushka's sufferings.

Fokine's reforms were the fruit of his concern to break away from the stereotyped attitudes of the Petipa works. Between the years 1904 and 1914 his ballets offered a remarkable exposition of these new ideas. He summed them up in the famous letter which he wrote to *The Times* in 1914 and in essence they comprise the following points:

1 The invention of a new form of movement corresponding both to the subject and the character of the music.

2 Dancing and gesture have no meaning in ballet unless they serve as an expression of dramatic action.

3 In general, to replace gestures of the hands (classic mime) by movement of the whole body.

4 A group of dancers is not merely an ornament. Fokine sought the expressiveness of the combined dancing of a crowd.

5 The alliance on equal terms of dancing with the other arts and the provision of liberty for the creative powers of the artists.

Fokine's career, however, was to receive a curious check. He had not reckoned with a fundamental characteristic of Diaghilev's nature – his almost obsessive search for novelty. The entire history of the Diaghilev Ballet (which became a permanent troupe under Diaghilev's guidance in 1911) is marked by a desire for new creators, new themes and new forms of expression. By 1911 Diaghilev was already concerned with moving on from the territory he had gained by the Fokine repertory. His love for Nijinsky impelled him to seek greater achievements for the dancer and in 1912 Vaslav Nijinsky composed his first ballet, *L'Après-midi d'un faune*. This was a complete rejection of the classic basis that underlay even Fokine's work. Inspired by Greek friezes, he sought a new language. The angle of the bodies of the faune and six nymphs, the walking steps which now replaced the academic vocabulary, were both simpler and more adventurous than anything that had gone before. *Faune* itself was a dead end; it implied, however, a completely new theory of what theatrical dancing could do, a theory which was completely stated in his third ballet *The Rite of Spring*. A revolution in both music and choreography, this ballet sought to evoke the past in a way far more truthful and elemental than had been conceivable even five years before. 'Turn in' as opposed to the classic dancer's 'turn out', heaviness in place of the lightness that was the aim of classicism, brutality instead of elegance or even exoticism: these were the ingredients of a ballet which shocked the artistic conscience of Europe both aurally and visually.

But Nijinsky was to leave Diaghilev in the year of *Rite* and though Diaghilev cajoled Fokine into returning, this was a stop-gap. By 1914 he had found a new young dancer, Leonide Massine, and the breakdown of the Ballet Russe activities brought about by the declaration of war in 1914 was the occasion for a final separation with Fokine and also encouraged the renewal of Diaghilev's experimental pattern: by 1915 Leonide Massine was embarked under Diaghilev's guidance as a choreographer. The experiments implicit in Nijinsky's work were forgotten. With Massine, a brilliant theatrical gift was encouraged and educated (Diaghilev throughout his career sought to school his protégés both in museums and through contact with some of the finest creative talents in Europe). Somehow the Diaghilev troupe managed to survive the war and Massine was launched upon that collaborative process that had proved so fruitful before 1914.

Diaghilev's obsession with the newest movements in art ensured that even during a world war the young Massine could work with Cocteau, Picasso and Satie on *Parade* (the first Cubist ballet). In Spain, an exploration of the country's culture was undertaken with Manuel de Falla, and, in conjunction with Picasso, resulted in *Le Tricorne*. Time spent in Italy was to produce the materials for *The Good Humoured Ladies* and *La Boutique Fantasque*.

After the successful return of the Ballet Russe at the war's end, problems crowded in upon Diaghilev. The old Europe which had provided such encouragement and financial support had gone, and in 1921 Massine quit the troupe. Without a choreographer at all, Diaghilev decided on the greatest gamble of his career, an opulent staging of *The Sleeping Beauty*. Produced with some of the greatest dancers of the age, and with the glorious designs of Léon Bakst, *The Sleeping Beauty** was presented in London in the fond hope that it would rival even the interminable run of *Chu Chin Chow* and allow Diaghilev to recoup his funds and prepare for the future. He had misread his audience. Accustomed to the short-breathed glamour of one-act ballets, unaccustomed to the classic dignity of Petipa, the London public soon tired of this magnificent staging. After 105 performances the Diaghilev troupe limped back to Paris leaving décor and debts behind. From this time we must date the dominance of French taste and French collaborators in the work of the Diaghilev company.

A refuge was found in Monte Carlo, but to please a fashionable audience Diaghilev was impelled to stage many lightweight novelties. The great innovator of the pre-war years now followed fashion rather than making it. Standards of presentation were maintained, the cream of French musical and artistic life was involved, but with the exception of a few crucial works the ballets staged were temporary delights.

A new choreographer was found in Bronislava Nijinska, sister of Nijinsky, and it seemed that with *Les Biches* and *Les Noces* the great pre-war days might have returned. *Les Biches* was an elegant and enchanting portrait of fashionable manners on the Mediterranean coast, redeemed from triviality by a choreographic language that exactly pin-pointed social and sexual manners. It was further enhanced by the unity of décor and music (by Marie Laurencin and Francis Poulenc), airy and witty.

Les Noces, on the other hand, was a profoundly serious evocation of the by now vanished world of holy Russian peasantry. In Lincoln Kirstein's words: 'Diaghilev provided an abrupt shift in taste for which a great part of his public was rarely prepared,'* but the bare and massive quality of the staging was a precise evocation of an ancient and deep-rooted peasant tradition. As in the case of *The Sleeping Beauty* the ballet did not find its truly appreciative public until many years later when it was revived by Nijinska for Britain's Royal Ballet and its truth became plain for all to see. (See Appendix B.)

The pleasant but entirely evanescent creations of the mid-twenties – who today remembers the choreography of *Barabau, La Pastorale, The Blue Train?* – might have suggested that the Diaghilev troupe had outlived its artistic function as anything but a talent to amuse. However the arrival of a group of émigré dancers from the Soviet Union in 1924 brought the young George Balanchine into the Diaghilev troupe. His choreographic talent, which had already declared itself in Russia, was first called upon to provide opera-ballets

* The original title *La Belle au Bois Dormant* was translated *The Sleeping Princess* in Diaghilev's 1921 production as in the Sadler's Wells Ballet's revival in 1939. The title changed to *Sleeping Beauty* when Sadler's Wells moved to Covent Garden in 1946.

* In his admirable *Movement and Metaphor: Four Centuries of Ballet*, Pitman, London, 1971, one of the most illuminating books on ballet for many years.

19

in Monte Carlo. There followed some lightweight pieces, typical of the Monte Carlo ambience, but in 1928 he was offered the recently completed Stravinsky score *Apollo*. In this Balanchine found his own identity and provided an identity for the classic ballet in the twentieth century (above all in America) which it bears to this day.

In August 1929 Diaghilev died in Venice. It was unthinkable and indeed impossible that his troupe should continue. In the light of after-events it even seems necessary that his death should have occurred with the end of the 1920s. With the scattering of his associates the seeds of the Diaghilev ideal were broadcast throughout the world; with the prestigious Ballet Russe no longer operating, smaller enterprises, as in Britain, could work without fearing direct comparison. It was possible for new forces to operate. Creators who had been through the Diaghilev academy were to shape the development of ballet throughout the West. Marie Rambert who had been with Diaghilev before the war, had opened a school in London; Ninette de Valois, a soloist with the Ballet Russe in the twenties, was also teaching and planning for the future in London: both these great women were to provide the impulse for the birth of British Ballet. In France, Serge Lifar, Diaghilev's last premier danseur, was to breathe life into the Paris Opéra Ballet. Lincoln Kirstein and Edward M. M. Warburg decided to give the classic ballet American expression and invited Balanchine to the United States to form a school and a company. During the 1930s and after, Massine and other Diaghilev artists were to perpetuate the Ballet Russe ideal in a series of touring companies that worked in Europe, Australia and America. The influence of these last troupes was ultimately to prove minimal, although during the 1930s the Ballets Russes were the most glamorous and popular of dance companies.

The 1939–1945 war was to mark a great divide in ballet. In Britain, Ninette de Valois had been able to found a company in 1931 at Sadler's Wells Theatre. During the pre-war years she had laid her foundations. She had acquired authentic versions of some of the greatest of the Imperial Russian classics; she had found a choreographer in Frederick Ashton, able to develop a native classic style; she had benefited from the musical and artistic counsel of Constant Lambert; her school was established; and in Margot Fonteyn and Robert Helpmann she had classic artists able to lead the company.

After the war years, when the company's popularity had been confirmed throughout Great Britain, the move to the Royal Opera House, Covent Garden in 1946 was to mark a rapid expansion of the Sadler's Wells Ballet. Today the Royal Ballet that Sadler's Wells became is one of the greatest companies in the world, sustained by its own choreographers and by the magnificent dancers produced by its own school, and with a repertory further enriched by ballets from the foremost choreographers of this century. Within a period of forty years, a completely sound national ballet tradition has been established.

Complementing this creation of a national ballet has been the activity of three other companies. The great achievement of Marie Rambert in pre-war years had been to discover and nurture young creative talent in both choreographers and dancers. Ashton, Tudor, Howard, Gore, Staff were among the choreographers who graduated from the Rambert nursery in the 1930s to larger opportunities elsewhere. Miraculously, Rambert could usually find successors but the economic problems which resulted from a need to tour during and after the war, playing to an audience eager for Tchaikovsky's ballets rather than the more sophisticated Rambert fare, brought the company to its knees. In 1967 the Rambert troupe was re-established with Norman Morrice (then Rambert's newest choreographic discovery) as co-director. The company's image reflected the influence of Nederlands Dans Theater (a Dutch troupe which had successfully combined classic and modern dance attitudes) and the new Ballet Rambert has since won tremendous acclaim – especially

A rehearsal of *The Sleeping Beauty* taken by Nicholas Sergueyev at Sadler's Wells Theatre in 1939. Robert Helpmann is seen as the Prince with members of the Sadler's Wells Ballet

with young audiences – for the freshness of its repertory and its awareness of contemporary trends in dancing.

The plight of the big touring company was exemplified in the repertory of Festival Ballet which was formed in 1950 as a showpiece for Alicia Markova and Anton Dolin. Initially dependent entirely upon box office receipts, the company offered middle-brow entertainment with a repertory that combined classic stagings – *Giselle*, *The Nutcracker* – with some revivals of Fokine and Massine ballets. These were often illuminated by guest stars from the old Ballets Russes companies. A partial subsidy was later provided by the Greater London Council to sustain enormously popular seasons at the Royal Festival Hall. Lengthy and very successful touring at home and abroad made Festival Ballet probably the most widely known of British companies. Nevertheless the uneasy financial conditions of the mid-1960s necessitated reorganization of the company. With a much increased state subvention, Festival Ballet has in recent years sought to encourage audiences to sample a slightly more adventurous choice of revivals and commissioned works in addition to the ubiquitous classic diet that still wins the company its largest audiences.

The idea of regional ballet in Britain owes much to the work of the late Elizabeth West who, with her choreographer – and then successor as director – Peter Darrell, made Western Theatre Ballet (originally based on Bristol in the West Country) an interesting new voice in Britain. The company's success was confirmed in 1968 when, with Arts Council support, it was transferred to Glasgow to become the Scottish Theatre Ballet.

In the United States, the plans laid by Lincoln Kirstein and George Balanchine in 1933, like those laid by Ninette de Valois in England, came to fruition in the immediate post-war years. The significant act was the invitation by Morton Baum to Balanchine to place his company in the New York City Center Theater in 1948. From this date, the New York City Ballet, as the company then became known, matured into the internationally famous troupe whose distinction is the richness of Balanchine's choreography. Just as the Sadler's Wells Ballet received the final accolade when it moved to the Royal Opera House, Covent Garden, so did the New York City Ballet find its grander setting when it moved to the State Theater, Lincoln Center, in 1964.

The Ballets Russes companies had fled Europe at the outbreak of war and found a home in the United States where they did much to popularize ballet. The post-war years, however, saw a decline in their activities: the de Basil company did not long survive Colonel de Basil's death in 1951; the René Blum troupe, by now the Ballet Russe de Monte Carlo, directed by Serge Denham (Blum died in a Nazi concentration camp), fell a victim to touring costs by 1963.

American Ballet Theatre, founded by Richard Pleasant and Lucia Chase (as an enlargement of the Mordkin Ballet) in 1939, started as a mammoth enterprise which aimed at the creation of an American repertory to be acquired from many distinguished choreographers, Fokine, Tudor, Howard, de Mille, Loring, and Nijinska. A huge roster of star dancers sustained the early years but soon, with the staging of Tudor's *Pillar of Fire* (1942) and the first ballets of Jerome Robbins (the first was *Fancy Free* in 1944) the company found an identity. The lack of a home theatre meant a fundamental insecurity and, having lost Robbins to Broadway, Hollywood and New York City Ballet, and with Tudor creating very few new works, the company has consequently tended to import creative talent rather than nurture it. Ever ready to engage foreign star dancers – Erik Bruhn, Carla Fracci, Natalia Makarova are examples – the company has kept its basic repertory in good repair. In recent years it has opted for classic stagings which have won an appreciative audience and by 1973 Ford Foundation money had given the company some measure of security.

Of the other numerous American companies – professional and semi-professional – the best known is the City Center Joffrey Ballet which took up residence at that theatre when Balanchine's company moved to the State Theater.

Any brief survey – such as this – of post-Diaghilev ballet in Europe and America must pay tribute to Diaghilev's last discovery, Serge Lifar, who moved to the Paris Opéra in 1930. During his twenty-eight years reign at the Opéra, Lifar revivified French ballet. His own choreographies may now no longer be popular, but they attracted (as did his dancing and that of the superb ballerinas he worked with) a new and eager audience to the Opéra. Serious attempts are being made to restore the troupe to its former glories, and the dancers produced by the Opéra school are still of superb quality.

Immediately after the Liberation of Paris, there was an extraordinarily rich period of young creativity, guided initially by Boris Kochno (Diaghilev's secretary and assistant) and the painter Christian Bérard. Two young choreographers, Roland Petit and Janine Charrat, and a remarkable generation of young dancers, gave a short but dazzling life to Les Ballets des Champs-Elysées during the late 1940s. In the mid-1960s André Malraux, the French Minister for the Arts, initiated the building of arts centres called Maisons de la Culture in an attempt to provide a lively arts tradition in the French provinces. At Amiens, and subsequently at Angers, the Ballet Théâtre Contemporain was initiated as a company dedicated to the staging of ballets which made use exclusively of contemporary choreographers.

In Germany, the pre-war modern dance tradition of Wigman and von Laban has been replaced by classic ballet. There are today ballet companies attached to all the major opera houses and in Stuttgart, particularly, the work of the late John Cranko provided Germany with a ballet company of international fame.

In Holland, the years immediately after World War II saw a great expansion in dance activity. The Dutch National Ballet has a wide-ranging repertory. From heavy reliance on traditional work, it is now moving into more adventurous territory. The Nederlands Dans Theater, founded in 1959, astonished Europe both by its productivity – averaging ten new ballets a year – and by the skill with which the modern and classic dance styles were fused in the choreography.

The major developments of ballet in Soviet Russia are detailed in Natalia Roslavleva's *Era of the Russian Ballet*. It was not until 1955 that the Western world was able to appreciate something of its achievements when the Moscow Bolshoy Ballet made its first visit to the Royal Opera House, Covent Garden. It is worth noting here, however, that although the Bolshoy and the Kirov

A general view of the Moscow Bolshoy Ballet's production of Lavrovsky's *Romeo and Juliet* with designs by Pyotr Williams, 1946

Ballet (from Leningrad) have since toured the world – and other Soviet companies have been seen – our view of Russian creativity is severely restricted since much of the native repertory has never been seen outside Russia. Nevertheless, the glamour of Russian Ballet and Russian dancers which, for the West, dates back to 1909, is still potent.

While ballet was being reborn following the death of Diaghilev, a parallel activity in the United States and in Central Europe was marking the important expansion of a free form of dancing. The expression 'modern dance' is the most usual term used to describe the vocabulary of movement that had been developed as a reaction against the classic ballet. It is not a precise description – ballet can be as 'modern' as any other form of dance – but the term is convenient and is generally understood and, with this reservation, we shall use it.

The first examples of modern dance are the works of Isadora Duncan and Loïe Fuller, but their influence was minimal. It is to the pioneering of Ruth St Denis and her husband Ted Shawn that the birth of modern dance in America can be traced. From their Denishawn schools emerged artists who first appeared in their company, propagating the gospel of free dance throughout the United States. The first generation of their students produced two influential practitioners, Martha Graham and Doris Humphrey. The vocabulary of movement developed in the Denishawn schools and companies was to be given

Martha Graham's *Cave of the Heart* with, left to right, Erick Hawkins, Yuriko, Martha Graham and May O'Donnell

an individual flavour and a very considerable extension by each of these women. This pattern of breaking away from one company to form an individual troupe and to develop an individual movement language is a continuing process in American modern dance.

Modern dance's concern with the ground as opposed to classic ballet's aspirations to lift the body away from the earth; the establishment and codification of a technique of training by Martha Graham and Doris Humphrey; the potent imagery with which they sought to explore psychological states through gesture: all this has provided a springboard for several generations of younger dancers and choreographers whose work may be a reaction against some of their ideas but, nevertheless, bears the impress of their systems.

At the same time in Europe a form of free dance had been explored by the German dancer Mary Wigman and the dance philosopher Rudolf von Laban. The example of their work was to be particularly strong in Central Europe, but its influence has not been lasting. Today's modern dance in Europe owes everything to the American tradition although Wigman's ideals were to be given American expression in the work of her pupil, Hanya Holm.

The second generation of true American modern dance has produced such artists as Merce Cunningham, Paul Taylor and – from the Humphrey school – the late José Limón. To these and many more is owed the present vitality of modern dance in both the United States and Europe.

From this brief look backwards and at current trends, we move on to a consideration of the elements of today's ballet. We do not pretend for a moment that our survey is exhaustive since each artist will have his own creative procedures. Our aim is to indicate the way in which certain creators work in order to illuminate the subject and encourage a deeper appreciation and enjoyment of dancing, both the dancing that owes everything to the traditions already discussed in this chapter, and the dancing that has moved so far away from the academic base that its debt, though real, may no longer be apparent.

The choreographer at work

'The structure of a ballet must be tight, compact, like the structure of a building; good ballets move in measured space and time like the planets.'

George Balanchine

We start this chapter with a statement which may seem an admission of defeat since we think it impossible to explain the creative process. To ask how or why of a composer or a painter or a choreographer is often to get the answer, 'I don't know'. In discussions with choreographers when we have said, 'we are writing a book about how a ballet is made', the reply has invariably been, 'I wish you'd tell *me* how it's done'. Nevertheless, there are certain procedures which enable them to start, and for all the choreographers whose testimony we have, making a ballet is a job of work, dependent upon the demands of a repertory, the need to produce a novelty for a season, the insistent requests of dancers for new rôles. Sir Frederick Ashton expects the muse to be in the rehearsal room at ten o'clock in the morning: 'If she deigns to look in all the better, but you have to get down and do the job – that's really what it amounts to.' (Covent Garden Book 15, A. & C. Black, London, 1965.)

George Balanchine concurs: 'In making ballets you cannot sit and wait for the Muse. Union time hardly allows it anyway. You must be able to be inventive at any time. You can't be like the cook who can cook only two dishes; you must be able to cook them all.' (George Balanchine, *Book of Ballets*, ed. Francis Mason, Doubleday, New York, 1954, 1968.)

The choreographer's craftsmanship, however, consists not only in being able to get on with the work but also in being able to create and fix the initial image that will spark off the choreography. Dame Ninette de Valois put the matter in a nutshell: 'There must be an image; it is the spirit behind all choreography; and once projected it is developed, or replaced by another that shows some form of progress in time. There must be, even in the most abstract of ballets, a

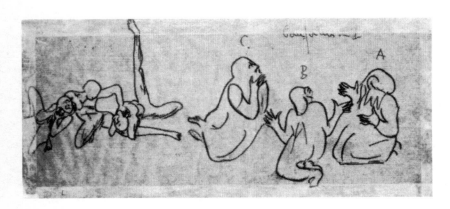

Page from Ninette de Valois' sketchbook for *Job* showing on the left Satan with War, Pestilence and Famine and, right, a group of the Three Comforters

The Comforters in *Job*

Harold Turner as Satan with War, Pestilence and Famine. This is the first production, designed by Gwen Raverat in 1931

sense of harmony, a sense of relationship between one passage and another.' ('Choreography 1973', by Dame Ninette de Valois.)

In making her ballets Dame Ninette has often had a very precise plan of work sketched out before she enters the rehearsal room. She uses little stick figures to illustrate the movements she intends to use. Her choice of subject-matter, which reflects her remarkable intellectual powers, encourages this approach: for *Job* there was a very detailed scenario; for *The Rake's Progress* the Hogarth paintings were faithfully reproduced on the ballet stage. This approach,

An engraving of one of William Hogarth's paintings for *The Rake's Progress*, 1735 – the Brothel Scene

The Brothel Scene from Ninette de Valois' *The Rake's Progress* ballet with designs by Rex Whistler, first produced 1935. David Blair, third from left, as the Rake

although it was the method of Petipa, is rare among today's choreographers. Sir Frederick Ashton for example has said:

> When I start rehearsals I have a fairly clear picture in my mind of what I have got to do – the story that has to be told, the characters that have to be created, the formal dances that have to be composed – I erect the scaffolding so to speak, and depend on my craft. All the composition, however, is done in rehearsal with the co-operation of the dancers. Sometimes the things I suggest prove to be the right things; the dancers try the steps; we all like them and we all think that they say what I am trying to say. Sometimes, though, I set an enchaînement which seems to me exquisite and wonderfully expressive, and the dancer finds part of it is awkward or 'wrong'. Then we take it all to pieces, and start again together. It may take a full month of rehearsals to set a single pas de deux, so that it flows easily and does not show ugly 'joins' between phrases. (Mike Davis, *The Royal Ballet*, Oldbourne, London, 1958.)

And George Balanchine in his *Book of Ballets* notes:

> Before beginning rehearsals I have an idea of what the general scheme of the ballet will be. I never arrange any of the dances or movements until I actually rehearse the dancers. I discuss scenery and costumes with the designer so that they will be in accord with the idea. I discuss the lighting, and I discuss the music with the composer and the conductor, but I don't discuss the ballet with my dancers unless we are doing a story ballet. I have no fixed

George Balanchine working with Violette Verdy of the New York City Ballet

29

Balanchine's *Serenade* was staged
by the Royal Ballet in 1964.
Balanchine is seen here at the dress
rehearsal with Svetlana Beriosova,
David Blair and (behind) Annette
Page

procedure. I don't come to rehearsals with any idea so definite and
fixed that it can't be changed on the spot.

I never write anything down. Often I try a step or a series of
movements on a particular dancer and then I change it to something
else. I indicate the steps first, and then the dancers repeat after me.
It is very simple to mount a ballet using dancers you have worked
with: they understand your smallest gesture and know what you
want almost instinctively. Sometimes I arrange the end of a ballet
first; sometimes I commence in the middle. Rehearsal time is
limited and I can't always indulge in the extravagance of following
the order of the music.

In her charming and evocative book *The Stravinsky Festival of the New York
City Ballet* (Eakins Press, 1973), the American critic Nancy Goldner gives a
precise description of Balanchine at work:

Here is a typical rehearsal. Balanchine walks into the studio and
smiles politely at the dancers. He asks the pianist to play a few bars
of music. Then he goes to one dancer and says softly, 'You do this.'
Sometimes he says, 'Maybe you do this,' but the 'maybe' suggests
less a tentativeness than a philosophy of never taking anything for
granted. He explains what he wants done by dancing it. The dancer
stands close to him and marks the movement or two as Balanchine
demonstrates. Then Balanchine moves to the next dancer or
gestures that everyone is to do the same thing, or that the next
dancer is to do the same thing but with the opposite foot and on the
next beat. Then the pianist plays the music, and the dancers dance
full-out. Balanchine watches the dancers. When they are finished
there is a pause of a few seconds, rarely more than thirty. Then he
walks over to a dancer (it could be the same one as before, or not)
and demonstrates another movement or two. If it's a turn, his

George Balanchine rehearsing
members of the New York City Ballet
in the second act of his *A Midsummer
Night's Dream*, 1962

finger twirls in the air. If it's a jump, he does a short-hand jump.
Most often he does what he wants to see. If the passage involves
partnering, he dances the male rôle. If the passage involves
complicated partnering, he dances the female's part too. If he does
not know what he wants by the time he walks the few paces from
the front of the room to the dancer, he pauses for a few seconds by
the dancer, his eyes lowered. One leg might inch a little forward, or
his arms might move almost imperceptibly. Then his head bobs
slightly, as if to say 'okay', and he shows the dancer what to do. In
the doing, he sometimes discovers that the movement feels
unusual. The dancers giggle and he smiles, but the dancers are
almost always able to reproduce what they see. If they cannot after
a few tries, Balanchine changes the step or makes a slight alteration.
Then the pianist plays the notes and the dancers dance the new
steps. After a few bars are choreographed, the dancers run through
all the steps for those bars. Balanchine does little correcting, except
for tempo. Problems iron themselves out as the dancers dance. He
leaves it to them to ask questions; more often they frown when
something is not smooth. He then repeats the step, emphasizing the
trouble spot with his body or with the kind of guttural utterances by
which musicians sing to each other. Toward the end of the
rehearsal, the dancers run through what they have so far learned.
During a two-hour period perhaps a few minutes of dancing have
been invented. After a few weeks, a ballet. The mechanics are
simple; the creative process invisible.

The choreographer's initial idea seems to come from various sources. Kenneth
MacMillan says:

Mostly I start with the music – music suggests an idea very often,
though with some works – *The Invitation*, *Solitaire* among others –

I found music to fit the idea. I had wanted to do a ballet about the Grand Duchess Anastasia after the Revolution and when I heard the Martinu *Fantaisies Symphoniques* my ideas jelled. When I listen to music a shape forms subconsciously so that when I go in to the first rehearsal I always think I have no idea what I am going to do. In fact, I find that I do know what I am going to do in a sense of shape though not of precise steps. I usually start with the pas de deux – I know exactly where it is going to come in the ballet. I do this because originally I found it very hard to write pas de deux, since as a dancer I was not a very good partner. I made myself do pas de deux and now it is out of habit that I start in this way. I always feel that the pas de deux must be the climax of the ballet and once it has been fixed it sets the style for the work. This was true even of *Song of the Earth* where I first of all composed the big duet of the final section.

Peter Darrell, the choreographer who did so much to create the initial image of Western Theatre Ballet (now Scottish Theatre Ballet), stressing always the 'theatre' in the company's title as much as the 'ballet', told us:

When one is an apprentice choreographer one wants to do ballets every week. When you are young you need to get your ideas out and then you can see which ones you are going to pick out and take forward – which are the good ideas and which are bad. You have to find your own style and I think I always knew that I was going to be a dramatic choreographer, rather than a 'steps' choreographer. I don't see how dance can be 'abstract' because it is so emotional: when you move an arm it is not abstract – it means something. Themes are always something one reads about or has an emotional response to. But 'true' in real life means nothing on stage and you have to translate, though you can't do that until you *know* the truth in real life. In my ballet *Home* I knew what the family felt, but I really wasn't sure with the inmates of a mental home that I had to show on stage, and so I had to make them up, and this failed because I wasn't being honest. I did a lot of homework and 'watching', for example, with *Mods and Rockers* in 1963 and I really researched the piece with a girl who made notes of what Mods and Rockers wore and did when we went to watch them in dance halls. But with *Home* there was not the time to do the proper research in a mental hospital. And this is something you can always tell, even if you try to cover up by bravura choreography. I am not a choreographer who prepares steps. I go into rehearsal to do the choreography because I know it – I feel it. Because I have an emotional approach, the emotion of my movement is what my dancers have to catch. When you begin to be a choreographer you learn the steps first of all, the language, and then you find the emotion. And then you marry them. In creating dances, that marriage for me comes in one moment of truth. That's why I need my dancers to watch me very closely in rehearsal. I do a step once and I've got the image, and if they haven't seen it I've lost it and I shall never be able to get back to that first clear shape. I can go back to what I was thinking but I can never quite recapture what it was. That, for me, is the important moment. If you are working with your own dancers they are attuned to this and they will catch the image and show you that they have got it, and then it's fixed. I work very much in a 'one' and this is the shape or key to the whole situation.

Peter Darrell rehearsing Gordon
Aitken in his production of *The Tales
of Hoffmann* for Scottish Theatre
Ballet, 1972

Peter Darrell's production of
Mods and Rockers for Western
Theatre Ballet, 1963

I get myself to the pitch where I want to do it – the movement must be natural – and when you do it first something seems to come right out of your soul. It is the act of creation; otherwise it becomes contrived. Thereafter you can work and shape what you have initially done, but it is that moment of giving birth that is vital. You have got the key and then you can work on the structure – that's simply a matter of craftsmanship. It is that first impulse which establishes the mood from which you can build a whole dance or a section. Sometimes in a solo it may be just the first step which is the *leitmotiv*.

The young choreographer Barry Moreland, who has worked both with the modern dance style of the London Contemporary Dance Company and with a large touring repertory troupe, Festival Ballet, states: 'I usually seem to start with a very slight pattern, though it is different with each ballet. This idea is sometimes just a phrase: if one wrote poetry it would be like a single image. One has to have a platform, a framework to start from, but I try to weave a very loose web when I begin choreographing and then I tighten it up.' He continues, 'I may set a few steps for a dancer who will stop when the phrase is completed; another will do it with such force that when the phrase ends the body continues almost inevitably and this gives a real stepping stone for the next section.' As this indicates, the choreographer in the rehearsal room ready to begin work is faced with an additional inspiration and challenge – the bodies in front of him. Whatever initial idea he may have, be it dramatic or a plotless realization of a score, the actual vocabulary of the ballet will depend to a considerable extent upon the artists he is using.

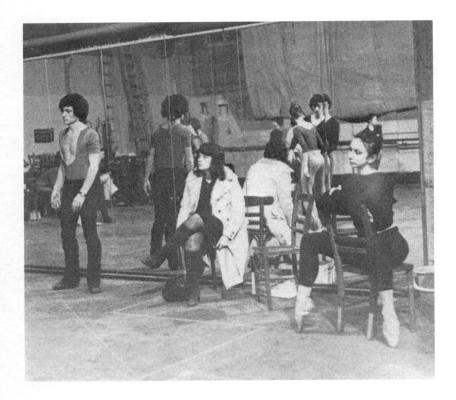

A rehearsal of Barry Moreland's *In Nomine* staged by London Festival Ballet for the Fanfare for Europe celebrations in January 1973 with, left to right, Barry Moreland, Nadine Baylis the designer, and Maina Gielgud

Kenneth MacMillan taking a
rehearsal of his *Images of Love* staged
by the Royal Ballet in 1964. Left to
right, Kenneth MacMillan, Desmond
Doyle, Nadia Nerina, Keith Rosson
and Anthony Dowell

Kenneth MacMillan notes:

I am inspired all the time by the dancers' bodies, by whoever works
with me; I have to find the right thing for their bodies. I tell my
cast very little at the beginning because I like to get the whole shape
of the music planned first; then I elaborate on the characterization,
and what I'm trying to put over . . . sometimes adding steps,
sometimes eliminating. I say very little at the beginning and I am
sure it is very puzzling to the dancers at first – and sometimes to me
too. I think I do this purposely, because I like my artists to find
themselves in their rôles. I do not like to lay down too many rules,
so I allow the dancers to improvise within the limitations imposed
by the steps and then we can go on from there.

As a choreographer I look in the main for musicality and
expressiveness of the body rather than a great technique, though I
am grateful if it is there, of course.

Obviously I respect classical forms. I think the classic dance has
infinite possibilities; it absorbs and then disciplines new impulses
and ideas. I feel this within my own work in that every day I will
set something and then say 'You can't do that'. With *The Rite of
Spring* I worked for three weeks and produced fiendishly difficult
choreography and then had to scrub the whole thing because I felt
it was wrong.

In considering the food for choreography, Barry Moreland makes the same
point as Peter Darrell. 'Choreography must spring from your own experience –
I don't see how it can be otherwise. One can attempt something outside one's
own experience but in the end it does not succeed just because it has not been
born from one's own feelings. I get very worried when I choreograph in an area

in which I have not had experience – there are certain emotions which one doesn't know and one gets very nervous, and one doesn't feel comfortable at work.' The distinguished American choreographer Paul Taylor agrees: 'I don't think creating is as much a matter of imagination with me as of real life. Everything that goes in to my work is from real life – I can't think of anything in my repertory that isn't factual. My subject matter is things I have noticed rather than things I have invented.' In a conversation with us during his 1973 visit to London, Taylor gave a most illuminating insight into his creative processes. He noted first of all that it was:

> different each time. It is very puzzling and very complicated. You can fall into patterns, but I keep trying not to do that. For a narrative work I think for a very long time about the story line, but for plotless pieces I find it is more a matter of working on the

A rehearsal in the Royal Ballet School of Kenneth MacMillan's 1962 production of *The Rite of Spring* with Monica Mason as the Chosen Maiden

An action photograph of the same scene in performance at the Royal Opera House, Covent Garden

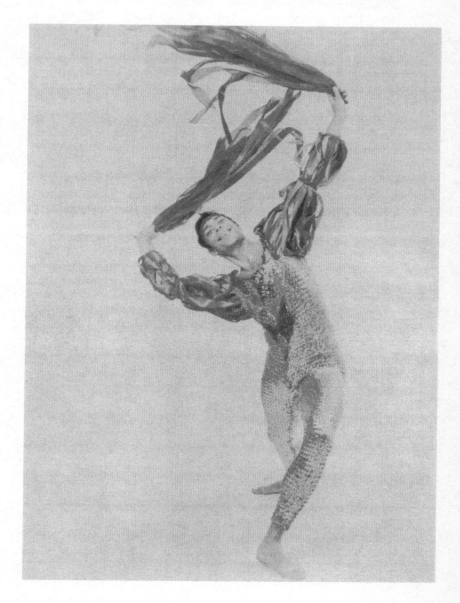

Paul Taylor in his *Book of Beasts*

37

dancers. Sometimes a dancer will give inspiration, but that's not necessary.

When I start a new work, I have to consider what other pieces are in the repertory and what will be suitable to go with them so that we don't have too many works of the same kind. And then I also have to think about which dancer in the company may need a special rôle. I try to set a ballet in about six weeks, to make a twenty to thirty minute piece. I may seem to get a lot done but I change so much that really it works out quite slowly. I come into the rehearsal early while the dancers are in class in the morning and I spend several hours before we get to the studio going over ideas and music, and working myself, and planning the day's rehearsal. When I am working on a dance for myself I find that it can be hard because one tends to be lazy, so sometimes I get another dancer to stand in for me, especially in the group work where I can't otherwise see the patterns. Any dancer will do, for it helps me just to see the steps on somebody else, but then I have to try to imagine that what they're doing isn't exactly what *I* shall do, so I usually set the dance on myself and then teach it to a dancer and see how it looks: choreography for myself takes me much longer than for other people because it's more guess-work.

Norman Morrice, director of the Ballet Rambert, when asked if he started with the score or an idea or the dancers' bodies, replied:

Up to now, all three. Very often it's been an idea I wanted to play with; occasionally, it has been a piece of music I'd like to move to; I may like a piece of music but if it doesn't make me want to move (although it might make the dancers want to) it is no good. I have no rules and regulations. The thing that terrifies me most of all is time: at some point someone says that we have to schedule a work and that scares me! I would like that ideal circumstance where I

Norman Morrice in rehearsal with the Ballet Rambert

Christopher Bruce with members of the Ballet Rambert in Norman Morrice's *Blind-Sight*, 1969

could 'play around' and every so often this would crystallize into a ballet. I sometimes start at the beginning of the score; I have sometimes started in silence, without music, or have started with a particular problem. In *Blind-Sight*, I played games for a few days as to what would happen with dancers who promised me that they would keep their eyes closed and wander around a room; then I gave them simple exercises or simple problems: to discover who they were, and could they find Jonathan Taylor in a crowded room. I find the structure the most difficult of all, because if you are working in a loose fashion, you can develop one part of a piece very easily and perhaps over-emphasize it, and when you assemble a long stretch of it, you find, in fact, that it hasn't a very good structure, that you have over-emphasized something and the rest of it isn't strong enough. I can enjoy being able to do something about that, but it is very difficult to throw away things that you particularly like: you have to discipline yourself as time goes by.

The bitter end is always the worst – it usually happens on the very last day; if it happens well, I'm happy; but doesn't always happen well. With *Blind Sight*, for example, the sort of comment I wanted to make was there but the actual kicking of the dead body came only on the last day.

As to influence on my work, Antony Tudor was the first big influence, then Ashton – I love the way his ballets are put together. Then Balanchine; then Martha Graham. She was the biggest

39

influence at the time when I was wanting to move into something other than classical steps. I distorted classical steps in my own way before that, but I wanted to find an interior kind of movement, which I couldn't develop myself except in a very eccentric way. In Graham's technique I found an interior possibility which changed all my feelings about balance and weight and, I suppose, at that time that was probably the biggest physical influence I had. These were guidelines.

Christopher Bruce, a principal dancer with the Rambert Company who is now also established as a choreographer, in discussing his early ballets, said:

I tend to start with movement ideas, emotional ideas which have some kind of effect on me physically and which I see in images of movement. After my second ballet, I decided that it was wrong for choreographers always to rely on a piece of music, or a poem, or even an idea coming from some other creative artist. I decided that, as a musician sits down and writes a piece of music that comes from *him*, a dancer should be able to do that and choreograph straight

Christopher Bruce rehearsing
There Was a Time for Ballet Rambert,
1973

Members of the Ballet Rambert in
Christopher Bruce's *Wings*, 1970

from his own instincts and emotions, and I made up my mind to try this. *Wings* was my third ballet, and it started from a movement idea with the music geared to what I wanted to do physically.

I had an idea about flight which was triggered off by a very brief section from Glen Tetley's *Ziggurat* in which the men become like birds. I thought this very strange and beautiful, and I asked Tetley's permission before I decided to develop it in to a ballet. I didn't fully appreciate where I was going – I knew that I wanted the shape of the ballet to start slowly, to build up, and then have a powerful ending which returned to the place it came from, a descent into a quiet finale. I had an image of the structure; and then I commissioned the music and worked with Bob Downes, tailoring the full score. At the beginning I remember thinking that one of the best things a choreographer could do would be to make a success of being economical, not making superfluous movement for movement's sake, though this might not be immediately apparent to the audience. I started with the image of flight, of a flock of birds, the men flying in, and I translated that into dance form. But these were dancers – men and women – being birds, so one had the dual image of birds *and* men. I ripped all the costumes because I wanted them to look as if they had been frozen in ice for millions of years, as if they were very old, with a sad weariness about them.

I even saw images of sad warriors, of birds dropping and being shot, even of a mass suicide like lemmings, a rite, a purge through which they had to go. I worked freely entirely from images and from what needed to follow next, theatrically and dramatically – all these things go through one's mind. It is very important for me to feel that a ballet is a 'total' piece; even if it is very simple, as long as it is complete and valid, then it is satisfying. I work instinctively, knowing and feeling.

41

Narrative and meaning

'What's it about?' 'It's about twenty-five minutes long.'

Barry Moreland

One is sometimes forced to think that mankind's first words were 'What does it mean?' Certainly as practising critics we are constantly faced with the need to explain where explanations are often impossible or unnecessary. This is a hangover from the nineteenth-century ballet's convention of impossibly complicated narrative that was expressed both in traditional mime and lengthy synopses. Since dance is a language which speaks directly to the eye it is a fault in the audience to expect a verbal message from movement. Ballets, of course, can tell stories marvellously well. Ashton's *La Fille mal Gardée* is straight narrative told in eloquent dance; MacMillan's *The Invitation* and *Las Hermanas* find potent dance imagery to translate a literary source into ballet; Balanchine's *Night Shadow* relates a Gothic incident in highly poetic form; Paul Taylor's *Big Bertha* is a danced short story of horrific power.

The choreographer in producing a dramatic ballet will first seek, reject and seek again, for a narrative which lends itself to danced expression. The inspiration for this may come from many sources. Kenneth MacMillan's *The Invitation* was inspired by two novels, *The House of the Angel* by Beatrix Guido and Colette's *Le Blé en herbe*, from both of which he drew elements to form his dramatic structure. Sir Frederick Ashton's *Ondine* was an adaptation of de la Motte Fouqué's story of the same title; his *La Fille mal Gardée* was based on the scenario of Dauberval's 1789 original. Roland Petit, like Jules Perrot before him, turned to Hugo's *Notre Dame de Paris*, and also used Rostand's play *Cyrano de Bergerac* for a scenario. Sometimes professional writers are approached by choreographers for dramatic structures, rarely with much success: the disastrous *Le Rendezvous Manqué* was based on an idea by Françoise Sagan, and in *Le Bal des Voleurs* Massine attempted a visualization of an Anouilh comedy. Western Theatre Ballet's desire for a new impetus for ballet brought plots devised by the playwrights John Mortimer and David Rudkin. Agnes de Mille's hectic *Fall River Legend* was inspired by the facts of the Lizzie Borden murder case.

In the twentieth century most of the inheritors of Fokine's methods produced works that might seem but brief dramatic incidents. It was in Soviet Russia that the tradition of full length ballets continued uninterruptedly across the great divide of the Revolution. The early post-Revolutionary years were spent in seeking themes that would express the new image of Russian society, and, after some searching *The Red Poppy* with its political message and slightly naïve dramatic structure, revealed the path ahead.

The development of the long Soviet ballet was considerably hampered by ideological problems – the Stalinist theory of socialist realism was a straitjacket from which Russian ballet is still extricating itself – but the wealth of Russian literature, especially the works of Pushkin, provided a rich seam for dance

* See Appendix E.

exploitation, as did the works of Shakespeare. (*Romeo and Juliet*, *The Merry Wives of Windsor*, *Othello* have all been successfully staged.) Thus Soviet Ballet, with its insistence upon drama, has found themes from literature both national and foreign (libretti have been adapted from works by Lope de Vega, Goldoni, and Georges Sand) and the very ideals of the Soviet state have also found an expression in ballets* which celebrate the achievements and the sufferings of the proletariat – *Flames of Paris* (the French Revolution), *Spartacus* (the revolt of the Roman slaves), *Laurencia* (Spanish peasantry), while *Path of Thunder*, based on a book by the South African author Peter Abrahams, highlighted the problems of apartheid. Igor Belsky's *Leningrad Symphony* is a searing portrayal of the sufferings of besieged Leningrad in 1942, and the achievements of astronauts and geologists are reflected in contemporary ballet. In the many republics that make up the Soviet Union, regional themes and dance styles also extend the range of dramatic subject matters. The Georgian choreographer, and one of the great dancers of Soviet Ballet, Vakhtang Chabukiany, has produced several works, like his three-act *Gorda*, inspired by the legends and history of his region.

In the West, the revival of interest in the three-act ballet initiated by Sir Frederick Ashton's work for the Royal Ballet, has turned choreographers' thoughts to the problems and rewards of long dramatic works that must also be satisfying as choreography. Sometimes these new full-length ballets have fed on past achievements. Ashton was forced by a shortage of scores to rework existing themes: *Cinderella*, *Sylvia*, *The Two Pigeons*, *La Fille mal Gardée* – his only commissioned score being from Hans Werner Henze for *Ondine*. His two artistic heirs, John Cranko and Kenneth MacMillan, have also developed the potential of the long narrative ballet; Cranko turning to *Eugène Onegin*, *The Taming of the Shrew* and *Romeo and Juliet*, while MacMillan also made a version of *Romeo* (the first Western choreographer to tackle the Prokofiev score was Ashton, for the Royal Danish Ballet in 1955) and then made a most adventurous exercise in translating history into dance in *Anastasia*. For Western, now Scottish, Theatre Ballet, Peter Darrell has composed three full-length dramatic works that were conditioned by the artistic ideals of his company: *Sun into Darkness*, *Beauty and the Beast*, and *Tales of Hoffmann*.

In all these large dramatic creations it is very important to appreciate the detailed structure, the placing, the pacing of incident, and the building of dance and dramatic effects. The problems of full-length ballets are enormous. Sir Frederick Ashton has spoken of the difficulty of finding a story which carries through, 'from the first act to the last. Otherwise you tend to get a story which fizzles out by the end of the second act and the third act simply becomes a series of divertissements or dances which keep the action going to the last minute. I tend to think that really the two-act ballets are almost the best because you get the whole thing a little more concise and more suited to the modern taste.' His *Ondine* in fact typifies the problems of the three-act work; the last act had to include a lengthy divertissement, while *La Fille mal Gardée* and *The Two Pigeons* were far more structurally tight, thanks to their two-act format.

John Cranko's *Prince of the Pagodas* was defeated by a plot which lacked focus, and even Peter Darrell's ultra-modern *Sun into Darkness* included a divertissement section. *Cinderella's* flaws are those of an unbalanced structure in which the first act is too long and the last act too short. It is the particular merit of Prokofiev's *Romeo and Juliet*, and one of its enduring attractions for choreographers, that its dramatic urgency never slackens and the adaptation of Shakespeare does not dissipate its momentum by being danced. It is worth noting that although Shakespeare's dramatic balance has been altered – the 'Ballroom Scene' in the play takes only a few lines whereas in the ballet it is a lengthy and crucial scene – the tragic power of the work has not been lost.

The twentieth-century dance's increasing insistence upon plotless choreography and upon works whose 'message' is nothing more (or less) than movement, has posed problems of understanding for an audience addicted to *Swan Lake*. A Balanchine ballet often exists as a visualization of its score; Glen Tetley's works can be very complex structures, filled with allusions and references to the human condition. In talking about 'meaning' in modern dance Paul Taylor said to us, 'It is important that a dance be a dance', and in the further matter of the constant inquiries as to the import of a modern dance gesture he observed very pertinently that ballet has an advantage, 'There is a tradition of ballet steps, and audiences don't ask "what does that battement mean?"'

In our experience we have found that most choreographers are perfectly happy for their audience to understand a ballet on whatever level they choose. Even when a text is involved, as in *Song of the Earth*, Kenneth MacMillan notes, 'I don't expect the audience to know what the words are about although I am pleased if they do. It doesn't worry me – my audience can take the ballet on any level. If they get the message of the words so much the better. Working with words, either directly as in *Song of the Earth* and *Images of Love*, or indirectly, as in *Romeo and Juliet*, I have to find a poetic image that will go with the words rather than illustrate them. Only in *Seven Deadly Sins* did I have to treat a text literally, because it clearly dictated all the action.'

In this matter of the audience's appreciation of a work's 'meaning', Norman Morrice speaks with great understanding:

> The choreographer has at some time got to make up his mind about the problem of the member of the audience who is going to see a work for the first time, and perhaps only once. It is always a difficult matter for me, because I hate dotting the 'i's and crossing the 't's. I feel that any ballet requires to be seen several times. I find it almost impossible to limit myself to making it sufficiently plain or obvious for a first viewing; but at the same time I can't

Members of the Ballet Rambert in Norman Morrice's *That is the Show*, 1971

44

Paul Taylor with members of his company in *Noah's Minstrels* as recorded for Granada Television in 1973

expect that every member of the audience is going to be able to afford or even want to come more than once. So one makes one's own choice and hopes for the best. If the movement is beautiful enough, you can catch them at once. I know that with other people's work I am often dumb. If I look at a piece and it attracts me at all, I know I am going to have to have the patience to see it again before I can begin to grasp it. It works the other way too. If I loathe a piece when I first see it, the loathing is such a positive thing that out of sheer curiosity I have to go and see if I shall loathe it as much, and often I then begin to like and admire it.

It can take a ballet company like the Rambert three visits, a year apart, to get an audience in a town to enjoy a certain work. There can even be a cross-fertilization between companies and audiences. Glen Tetley's *Field Figures* for the Royal Ballet, premièred in Nottingham, was well received because Rambert had been there for three years running, with a Tetley repertory.

The young English choreographer Richard Alston is much concerned with experiment in the theatrical function of dancing and in the possibilities of movement, and he may be conveniently called a member of the avant-garde. But his work is very closely structured and as seriously considered as that of any of the other choreographers we have consulted. The bugbear of meaning affects him too. He commented: 'I usually don't say anything about a piece to my dancers until it is finished. But once the movement is completed I can tell

Richard Alston in his own *Who is Twyla Tharp?* performed in 1971 at a Festival Ballet workshop

Celeste Dandekar and Linda Gibbs in Richard Alston's *Lay-Out* as performed by the London Contemporary Dance Theatre in 1973

Members of the London
Contemporary Dance Theatre in
Richard Alston's *Lay-Out*

them what they are doing. Often, if the piece is strong enough, the idea comes across anyway, but there is also the fact that one never really completely understands a work oneself until after seeing it three or four times in performance, simply because one is so bound up with it; unless – for me at any rate – there is such a set structure and atmosphere in the score (created by someone else) that I understand what they have done, and know what I want to do with what they have created. But working without music or on an idea of my own, it takes probably four performances to see what I have done and then I can sometimes see gaping holes.'

Antony Tudor is one of the most precise craftsmen in the fixing of emotional nuance and seemingly one of the least communicative to his artists in rehearsal. Anthony Dowell, when rehearsing *Shadowplay* with Tudor, noted, 'At one time I literally didn't know what he wanted from that rôle and he would only say, "You must just dance it as I set it and nothing must creep in".' (*Dance and Dancers*, April 1969.)

We have talked here of the creation of 'plotless' dances, but Tudor brings us inevitably to the consideration of character and psychology. As Jerome

Antony Tudor rehearsing
Anthony Dowell for the Royal Ballet
production of *Shadowplay*

Antony Tudor rehearsing
Shadowplay which he staged for the
Royal Ballet in January 1967

Anthony Dowell as the Boy with
Matted Hair in Tudor's *Shadowplay*
with the Royal Ballet

Robbins said: 'Tudor brought psychological motivation into ballet; he conveyed through movement emotions that could not be put into words.' On this very point Kenneth MacMillan observed: 'There are lots of things ballet can't do – as Mr Balanchine said "There are no sisters-in-law in ballet" – but one can show relationships if they are carefully worked out beforehand.'

An invaluable study of Antony Tudor's work is to be found in two issues of *Dance Perspectives*, numbers 17 and 18, in the second of which Selma Jeanne Cohen assembles some remarkable testimony from Tudor's closest interpreters and associates. She writes:

> The dancer as character may contribute movement ideas to Tudor choreography. But as a dancer he is never allowed to 'interpret' a movement. Margaret Black, Tudor's assistant at Julliard says, 'In Tudor's choreography you never have to super-impose feeling. You don't have to make the movements speak: it does,' and Diana Adams elaborates: 'Tudor does not want interpretation; he wants simplicity of execution. When he refrains from telling a dancer verbally about her rôle, it is because he does not want her to be influenced by her personal feeling about the character. The movements itself should suffice, without interpretation being added to it.'
>
> Tudor's dancers have noted how he conveys characterization by giving them 'key movements'. His characters are conceived, not as mental ideas, but as physical images; each is based on a movement concept. Thus, Tudor seldom describes a character by talking about it; he demonstrates the movements and the dancer has to take it from there. Hugh Laing calls attention to the key movements in *Pillar of Fire*: for the younger sister a toss of the head; for Hagar, pulling at her collar; for the elder sister, putting on her gloves, patting Hagar, pulling back into the formality of the New England spinster; for the young man, a sharp thrust with one leg, a plié, and an arrogant straightening.

Hugh Laing, outstanding Tudor dancer, writes:

> You can't be a dancer in Tudor ballets. Everything is based on classical technique, but it must look non-existent. The structure is emotional; the technique is twisted, disguised. The flow of the movement-phrase must never be broken, and this is what makes his choreography so difficult technically. He may want – and expect you to be able to do – four pirouettes, but you can't let the preparation for the pirouettes show. The turns are part of a phrase that may be saying 'I love you, Juliet', and you must not interrupt that phrase to take a fourth position preparation, because then you are paying attention to yourself as a dancer and not to Juliet.
>
> Tudor sometimes seems hard and vicious, but he has respect for his performers. You are not his tool; his string-pulling lets you be alive on the stage. You must be serious and dedicated, because he demands that you enter completely into a rôle. Once he knows you understand the character, he will trust you creatively. He never set my final walk-off – now a quite famous one – in *Pillar of Fire*. I knew there had to be something vulgar and nasty in it, and something of the arrogance of a strutting sailor. So I just walked, with hips tight and shoulders up, and Tudor said that was just right.
> (*Dance Perspectives*, no. 18.)

Nora Kaye and Hugh Laing in Antony Tudor's *Pillar of Fire*, 1942, for American Ballet Theatre. The picture illustrates the stance to which Laing refers in the text

'I never tell my dancers what a piece is about,' says Barry Moreland.

> 'If they ask "what's it about?" I usually say "well, it's about twenty-five minutes long". Dancers who know me well just do the movement, and towards the end they say: "It's about . . ." and I can usually see what it's about, and I can start to explain. Often, I will only see what a piece is "about" when it is finished, though

sometimes when you are working on a dance you may be reading and your eye picks up something which relates to what you are doing. This happened for example with the Seferis quotation I use for *Summer Solstice*. I don't think one needs to tell a dancer much about what you are doing. When I was a dancer I never asked. Sometimes dancers do ask, and so you tell them, and they then start to appliqué a whole story onto a variation, acting like crazy. You have to keep a tight hand on interpretations and thus on the ballet.'

The ballets of Glen Tetley have sometimes presented problems to those members of the audience who inquire persistently for meaning rather than accepting the dance on its own terms. We talked with Tetley about his whole process of creation and in his comments we hope that some guidelines emerge for a proper appreciation of his ideas. He admits first of all that he is 'incredibly influenced by the music'.

Alain Dubreuil, Gaye Fulton and Dudley von Loggenburg in Barry Moreland's *Summer Solstice* as staged by London Festival Ballet in 1973

When I made *Pierrot Lunaire*, my first ballet, I had had the score
for about ten years before I found the courage to do it. I did a very
long preparation for it, listened for a long time, because I find music
crucial to me. Though I work in very different ways from when I
started fifteen years ago, I am still very, very conditioned by the
score.

I have a very visceral reaction to Stockhausen. It is not music I
feel that anyone can sit down and listen to – for me it is not that
kind of music, unless you are in a special kind of condition or if you
are involved in it for work. In general I don't listen to the kind of
music I work with for relaxing. When I like a score very much I
purposely put it away until I begin to work with it, because I feel
one can deaden one's responses to music and I want it to 'hit' me as
if I had never heard it before.

I start a ballet at the beginning, but I never know precisely where

Niels Kehlet of the Royal Danish
Ballet in Glen Tetley's *Pierrot
Lunaire*. The ballet was first performed
in New York in 1962

Glen Tetley rehearsing Willy de la Bije and Jaap Flier of Nederlands Dans Theater in his *The Anatomy Lesson*, 1964. The photograph was taken during the BBC television programme about the ballet

it is going to land up. I find that the curious thing is that one is like a multiple tape-recorder. You take in impressions all the time that are stored away for ever: tactile things, visual things, sounds, images from everywhere. When I come to work on a ballet – if I am working in the right way – scores I have loved, incidents, things suddenly make connections that I never put a connection to before: sometimes there comes a wonderful state when everything starts to have meaning for me, and I try not to follow a 'message' or a particular pattern that has been pre-determined. I can go into a work as a 'that moment' exploration of what I am doing. And if I am working intuitively, if I have intuitively responded not only to music but also to the dancers I have chosen, then things come together and actually everything *does* have meaning. There is a structure to all things.

If I said 'this is what the ballet means', it would be very hard for me to verbalize it. It means a lot of things that do not have a verbal image and have a much more dimensional image than words. I express it in a physical way. That's why we do ballets: if I had a message I'd write it.

Rag Dances, for example, started with Oliver Messiaen's score, the *Quatuor pour la fin du temps*, which came from a prison camp. That was a starting point. I was very struck by the score on all levels. I liked it for its religious element, but the ballet came out of a

53

New York situation, which can be like the biggest prison camp in the world. Four of my friends had died within four months of each other, and there are four images of those people in *Rag Dances*, people who were very close to me, and very specific images, wildly taken out of context; but the stimulus came from that. As to the ballroom dancing couple: in a passage in the Messiaen score there is an image of Christ descending, and I associated it in a strange way with ballroom dancing because of the vamp quality in the music he wrote, and because for me, as a child, ballroom dancers were god-like, the most beautiful people I had ever seen, unlike the rest of us struggling along and having problems, but far removed and above us – Fred Astaire and Ginger Rogers! They floated across humanity. Also, the figure of the God in church had, at that time, a tinsel image which disturbed me, and yet there was something beyond it which was so vast. I wanted this section to be absolutely pure: those are the salvation elements that we hang on to. It may not be the greatest symbols which save us, but something that relaxes the whole pattern.

As to my choreographic language, I came into dancing very late – I was twenty – and I was not indoctrinated into one particular theory. I always had a deep physical feeling for classic ballet – the first dance I saw was classic ballet – but I grew up in a period when modern dance had a tremendous highpoint in America. The experience I had with Hanya Holm and Martha Graham and Antony Tudor was of my own choice because I felt I needed all of those aspects, and when I use classic or modern technique or combine them, to me, it is all part of one thing: I don't categorize and I don't feel strange. It feels very natural to me. I find all of my stimulus in bodies: I wouldn't want to choreograph if I weren't stimulated by people.

The dancer's contribution

'A choreographer, though possessing the same emotions as other creative artists, has no way of expressing himself but through movements which he must implant in the muscles of other dancers.'

David Lichine, *Ballet*, September 1947

'Choreographic movements are the basic movements which underlie all gesture and action, and the choreographer must train himself to discover them. It is necessary for the choreographer to see things which other people do not notice.'

George Balanchine, *Dance Index* no. 11

Of great importance in analyzing the creative process is the contribution made by the dancer. No choreographer has ever imposed his will utterly upon his interpreters; the majority – as the testimony we have assembled already shows – feed enormously from the bodies and temperaments of their cast. No dancer would be so arrogant as to say they had 'made' a choreographer, but none would deny that their contribution to a ballet is very real. The sort of exchange of inspiration that seems most remarkable is that which occurs when a creator finds a dance muse as Fokine did in Tamara Karsavina, as Ashton found in Margot Fonteyn, as Balanchine has repeatedly done throughout his long career with a series of ballerinas, and as Kenneth MacMillan has with Lynn Seymour.

The relationship is sometimes the result of an instinctive rapport, sometimes a breakthrough has to be made. Tamara Karsavina, in her incomparable book of memoirs, *Theatre Street*, confesses that although at first 'Fokine's intolerance often pained and shocked me . . . his enthusiasm, his impetuosity, subjugated my fancy. My belief in him was deeply rooted before he actually began producing. Through casual remarks of his, through tirades steeped with a feeling of a crusade to be led against the smug and the Philistine, there loomed new shores, there called glorious exploits.' The collaboration between Ashton and Margot Fonteyn – the longest of its kind in ballet history – began less easily. Ashton has recalled:

> When Margot was first pointed out to me as ballerina material I was unable to find much inspiration in her. I was conditioned to Markova's sharpness and precision in dancing and, compared to all that brittle delicacy and finesse, Margot was not impressive to me. She had weak footwork and in some way she did not use her body properly. There was no doubt that she was the most promising of the young dancers at that time, but there seemed to be a constant tussle in all my early contacts with the young Margot.
>
> When finally I created for her the rôle of The Bride in *Baiser de la Fée*, I felt a great frustration in being unable to mould her precisely as I wanted. Her performance needed to be much more precise. I got very cross with her at times and went on and on at her relentlessly. One morning after I had been particularly severe, she suddenly rushed and threw her arms around my neck and burst into floods of tears. I knew then that I had won the battle; that I would be able to work with her. (*The Art of Margot Fonteyn*, photographed by Keith Money, Michael Joseph, London, 1965.)

From Dame Margot's viewpoint:

> At first I thought he was absolutely mad, because he kept asking for quite impossible movements which I had never been asked to do before. I remember running home and complaining and saying that I couldn't possibly do the things he expected.
>
> But no matter how impossible the things he expected, he was always able to do them himself. He was very supple and plastic in his movements and he didn't seem to have any bones at all and he would throw himself round the studio and do some twists and turns and quick little steps and then look rather exhilarated and say, 'now do what I did.' To which we'd say, 'well, what did you do?' And he'd try to do it again, probably rather differently. (Zoë Dominic and John Selwyn Gilbert, *Frederick Ashton, a Choreographer and his Ballets*, Harrap, London, 1971.)

On working with a choreographer Lynn Seymour says:

> It's different every time – the more you work with someone, the easier it is for you though not necessarily for the choreographer. You come into the rehearsal as a kind of empty sponge, and wait to get the vibrations from the music and the 'tone' of the steps. With Kenneth MacMillan this is what he sets up and then you start getting the idea. He will perhaps just say 'I had this sort of idea', and you will listen to a piece of the music and he will then show something and say 'Like this' or 'Why don't you start over there

Frederick Ashton rehearsing Margot Fonteyn and Rudolf Nureyev for a sequence in the documentary film *Margot Fonteyn* which included a rehearsal sequence of *Birthday Offering* filmed at the Royal Opera House. *Birthday Offering* was created by Ashton in 1956 to celebrate the twenty-fifth birthday of the Royal Ballet; Fonteyn danced the principal ballerina role

Svetlana Beriosova as the Tsarina
and Lynn Seymour as the Grand
Duchess Anastasia in the little
Russian dance in the first act of
Kenneth MacMillan's *Anastasia* for
the Royal Ballet, 1971

* See Appendix A.

and dash over here?' And you try it. He doesn't name steps but he
gives examples. And the problem usually becomes to translate this
idea into the rhythmic form that the music has, and make it
possible. This seems to be the thing that I have been best at and I
do it for MacMillan. I may say 'I'll do this – a quick one here and a
slow one there', and he'll look at it and say 'Yes; well, maybe if you
do this instead of that, or try it on the other leg, or bend here', and
that is how we seem to put it together. Of course, there are other
times – like the little Russian dance I do in *Anastasia* just before the
Tsarina joins me – which went very smoothly and was all done in
about fifteen minutes.

With *Anastasia*'s last act (which was the first to be made – it was
a separate ballet he staged in Berlin in 1968) we had been reading a
lot about Anna Anderson and MacMillan told me quite a lot. So we
started off with the three major characters; the man, me, and Vergie
Derman who was playing all the other characters. We started at the
beginning and MacMillan said, 'We'll begin with you fascinated by
the floor, because it is the only real thing that you can hang on to.'
So that all the walking at the beginning is just trying to keep on the
floorboards and touching them – it's a question of identity; then
comes the waving to the crowds – that flowed quite easily, and there
was a movement with one of my hands masking the other which we
did as a joke against Monica Parker, our Benesh* notator, because
it was the one movement that she said was awkward to write down.
That is how we started out on that scene. There followed the pas de

deux which were really difficult, because MacMillan wanted to use Rudolf Holtz's strength (he was the man) as much as possible so that the double work became very strenuous. I think MacMillan has visions, especially with pas de deux, and sometimes they are impossible because he expects your knees to bend forward. He did in *The Invitation*. But then something comes out of that, simply because your knee doesn't bend in that way and another movement evolves. The most exciting part is working with a partner. When I work with Donald MacLeary, who is a marvellous artist, things just seem to happen. He would start a movement and it would change into something else and MacMillan would say 'That's lovely' and take over from there. In *Baiser de la Fée* the Mill scene flowed very easily. MacMillan showed us what he wanted and the beginning came really very fast. But the solo took quite a time – it was tricky, and we worked on that for ages. I had a vision about it because MacMillan had me starting with big, élancé jetés and I visualized melting out of them in a more modern way which became a kind of trade mark, and we used it a great deal. When MacMillan created *Romeo* all the pas de deux flowed, and I remember when we came to the rehearsal for the bedroom scene MacMillan had it all planned. I was to sit on the bed quite still. Kenneth MacMillan was afraid to do it because he felt that people might say there wasn't enough dancing – that seemed a real concern to him – but he dared. Even though choreography is always there, you sometimes discover what is really in it much later on. I did so with the last act of *Romeo*, when I found recently that there is something abandoned in Juliet's desperation.

By the time we have broken the ice in rehearsal we have millions of ideas. MacMillan sets the tone and the basis and then we take off from there – it is a partnership.

Lynn Seymour also worked for Frederick Ashton in *The Two Pigeons*.

The first thing we did was a little variation in Act I, which was very difficult. We did the steps right away because Sir Frederick had plotted what the shape of the floor pattern was going to be and he would say, 'Now we want a step that goes across here and then one that goes back and around.' And he divided it like that and it was plotted like that. He showed me a step and I would do it – he had a very set conception and the whole thing was worked out. There were steps that I thought would not suit me at all but he made them right. He would say, 'I want to show your feet off,' or 'Pavlova used to do this', and he would show me some of her steps and I would copy that. I remember that the last act pas de deux went very easily: he wanted my feet out and lots of ports de bras. It was the thing he did last and with that lucious music he could hardly wait to get to it.

Lynn Seymour has also worked for Glen Tetley, and Tetley pays warm tribute to her. He says:

Lynn Seymour is a paramount example of a dancer who seems to have no beginning and no end. The movement is endless. Lynn has this quality, and it is what I have always loved in dance myself – not the collection of photographs, the dance that stops. I like best the intuitive dancer who knows how to link everything, who puts in so

Vergie Derman (left) and
Deanne Bergsma of the Royal Ballet
in Glen Tetley's *Field Figures*, 1971

much movement as Seymour does, as Marilyn Williams of Ballet
Rambert does, as Mea Venema with Nederlands Dans Theater
does, as Deanne Bergsma of The Royal Ballet does.

I start something, and then the dancer carries it on. Because of
my background and training in America (besides technique, we had
improvisation, composition, etc.) I work a lot through improvisation
myself, then I turn it over to dancers, and when they ask 'Will you
repeat that?' I say 'I won't' because I want to see what they will do
with it. With *Field Figures*, because of the Royal Ballet's structure,
the division of classes of boys and girls, the immensity of the
organization, the enormous distances, even between me and the
dancers in rehearsal, I wanted to break that down, even the
permissible distance between dancers in classic ballet; and it was a
point of working for me and for the dancers, to change their
established patterns of rehearsal.

I started from there, entwining the dancers as closely together as
I could, and because of the classic dancer's usual dependence upon
musical phrase, I didn't start working with music for quite a while.
We worked only with movement; they were a bit unnerved by that,
and then the score became a marvellous 'other thing' that came
into it, which either amplified it or in some way pulled the phrasing
down, or expanded it. I wanted to do a work in which the audience
would just watch and be fascinated by movement for its own sake.
That is the wonderful thing of working with dancers in a studio and
what you are involved in there: one must be inspired by their
movement.

In the interdependence of choreographer and dancer much devolves upon their
emotional understanding of each other, quite as much as on the choreographer's
physical conception of a dancer's powers. Peter Darrell demands close attention
from his artists in first setting the mood of a scene (see p. 32). His dancers know
from the very first what he expects of them in regard to his method of work, and
Darrell's own dependence upon his dancers can often initially spring from his
understanding of the emotional inflections they can give him. In connection
with this he says:

Working with one's own dancers is the ideal. You know what they
are going to give you and they know what they are going to get
from you, and that is a marvellous relationship, because when you
go into rehearsal you have an immediate rapport. They know what
you are talking about and I find that I 'take' from them a great deal.
With a strange company you have to work harder, because you have
to discover your dancers – which is why the best choreography
always comes from working with people you know. It is not so much
a problem of working with bodies, but with personalities. You can
see a lovely body and think that you would like to create on it,
because you can get this or that from it; but with personalities, you
really need to be with them for a couple of months before you know
what you can do with them. You can tell within a couple of days
what a person can do physically, and that is important; what you
can't get is what they can do for you. You can develop their line, or
extensions, or turns; it is whether they will *understand* what you are
saying that matters.

Norman Morrice noted that early on in his career he composed a considerable
amount of his choreography on his own body first of all. Nowadays he says:

I still do a lot of it on my own body. I now find, though, you can
get such exciting things by sitting back at a given moment and
saying 'just come from there to there, and if you were feeling such
and such, what do you think you might do?' And suddenly the
dancers do something quite extraordinary.

I am working with dancers some of whom I have known for many
years: the challenge is to push them forward. That is why with the
Rambert company I feel it is so important to have outside
choreographers every so often, because I am trapped in a situation
where sometimes I think I know so much about a dancer that I am
inclined to label them. An outside choreographer comes along and,
through a different process from my own, provides something
enormously exciting about a dancer, and my own interest is
immediately developed. It is a big trap in some ways when you
know the dancers so well. The new view of a body feeds you.
Though, of course, when you know dancers well it has a great
advantage; if you have a particular kind of movement or emotional
drive that you want out of a rôle in a ballet, you automatically know
who is going to be the best dancer for that.

Sometimes I tell my dancers the whole story of a ballet, but that
can be dangerous because then they get preconceived ideas about it
– though it is unfair to keep them in the dark too long. But dancers
can start to give you emotions you don't want – you have to control
their emotional response. Choreography can be ruined by an
'acting' façade put on top of it: it can become quite sickening. I
always find impossible that awful moment when dancers decide that
they are going to woo an audience. There are some ballets where it
is necessary to take the audience into your confidence with a raised
eyebrow, but nine times out of ten I loathe it. The separation
between 'them' and 'us' is destroyed by one performer who is
indulging in this kind of personal relationship with the audience.
That's when I think 'now we really should be talking to them'.

The separation means illusion of course; behind the proscenium
arch and the orchestra pit there is a magic world that you can use.
In the situation of the Young Vic (a thrust stage in the round), that

magic no longer exists and when the company appeared there we had to find a totally new relationship with the audience which was based upon a kind of simplicity, with the dancer not being this fabulous creature set apart but a person, directly involved with the audience, who is incidentally a dancer. One of our dancers said, 'It is the first time I have felt like *me* on stage,' because he was only six inches from the audience, and there was no way of being anything other than what he was, no possibility of acting. I found the dancers measured up very well to being dancers/people instead of dancers/performers – but it strips them very bare.

A totally different approach to the dancer's contribution comes from Paul Taylor who had the distinction of being invited by Balanchine to create a solo in *Episodes*. Taylor, speaking both as dancer and choreographer, appreciates the enormous craft that sustains Balanchine's creativity. 'Balanchine has an ability, through necessity, to work quickly. You've got to learn exactly what he wants and I had three rehearsals with him for my solo in *Episodes*. He would show me two or three movements at a time. He demonstrated what he wanted and he choreographed it completely. There was something to do on each count but, at first, it was like a crossword puzzle and it was very concentrated. It was all very formal. There was no talking or chatter. Balanchine does not give you verbal images. It's not a mental process – it's a purely intuitive, physical thing with time, shape and movement.'

Taylor's testimony is evidence once again of a very remarkable quality of Balanchine's choreography, in particular its relationship to its interpreters. Balanchine's steps are self-sufficient; they do not depend upon individual mannerisms, or even on one particular style (although his own New York City Ballet obviously gives the most authentic readings). Balanchine seems to show little interest in what is called 'temperament' or star quality or the affectations with which indifferent dancers bolster their inadequacies. As he says 'I don't want soul'. The American dancer and choreographer Dennis Nahat, talking to the magazine *Dance and Dancers* in May 1972, observed that, 'Where Balanchine is so great is that everybody can do his ballets. He sends them out to everybody and the construction is so strong that they last. What happens with many choreographers is that they do ballets suited only to particular people and they can not be done by anyone else.' Nahat's point is crucial in considering the creative methods of choreographers and the life-span of ballets. It is a commonplace of criticism that much of the Diaghilev repertory is travestied in present day revivals. *Le Spectre de la Rose*, for example, *should* be unthinkable without Karsavina and Nijinsky, for whom it was created. *Le Tricorne* is but a shadow of itself without Massine as the Miller. *Marguerite and Armand* is unimaginable without Fonteyn and Nureyev. Roland Petit's *Carmen* has shown itself to be insupportable without Renée Jeanmaire's physical magic. And we would utter a plea for the final death of Pavlova's swan who has been too long a-dying. Ballets are often vehicles, designed to exploit the qualities of a dancer. The more serious the star, the more valid this vehicle may become, and here the choreographer is very much like a tailor fitting the choreographic suit of clothes exactly to the dancers' requirements. A case in point is the beautiful *Nomos Alpha* that Maurice Béjart composed for Paolo Bortoluzzi, which explored the gifts of this outstanding dancer in superb fashion. Diaghilev first showed stars could be made without indulging them. Indulgence may seem the correct description for his initial presentation of the unique artist Nijinsky, but Diaghilev understood Nijinsky's qualities, and in a series of exotic rôles which he had made for him, he enhanced his greatness. Significantly, once Nijinsky was without Diaghilev's guiding affection he was lost.

We do not wish to seem graceless and ungrateful to dancers, but we approach here the very serious problem of the erosion of choreography. Until recent years choreography has survived entirely upon the physical transmission of steps.* Often a ballet may depend for its effect upon the most subtle inflections of movement, and upon a style that has only been achieved at the end of weeks of concentrated rehearsal. In a repertory company it is extremely difficult for dancers to adjust themselves to perhaps three different styles in an evening, and inevitably subtleties which give the whole quality to the piece will disappear.

* See Appendix A.

The question of stylistic authenticity is very important. No-one but the Royal Danish dancers, who do a Bournonville class every week, can present all the delicate inflections of that great master's choreography although many companies now attempt Bournonville fragments. Conversely, the Royal Danes failed to understand the style of Ashton's *La Fille mal Gardée*, a ballet for which they would seem ideally suited. Yet MacMillan's *Romeo and Juliet*, created for Britain's Royal Ballet, gained in dramatic power when staged by him for the Royal Swedish Ballet, because a deeper stage in Stockholm seemed to frame the tragedy more effectively, and because the lengthy dramatic traditions of the company encouraged them to bring MacMillan's characters alive. The rôle of Juliet has also cast some light on this question of the dancer's response to a rôle. It was written for Lynn Seymour, an intense lyrico-dramatic dancer, and every impulse in the action, every outline of the choreography sprang from her body. Margot Fonteyn's performance in the rôle was totally unlike this and seemed more a presentation of Shakespeare's Juliet than MacMillan's.

Dancers, of course, can often justify inadequate works and make them not only bearable but positively enjoyable. This can be equally true of an indifferently written rôle or of a thoroughly mediocre staging. The Bolshoy Ballet's rickety old *Don Quixote* is made to seem one of the joys of the theatre if Ekaterina Maximova and Vladimir Vasiliev are dancing. Indeed, it seems all too common in Soviet ballet to find miraculous dancers redeeming far from miraculous ballets. Olga Lepeshinskaya (who graduated from the Bolshoy's school in 1933 with the rank of prima ballerina) not surprisingly gave the three-act *Mirandolina* most thrilling life, and Grigorovitch's *Spartacus*, with its very uneven qualities, is required viewing for the performances of Mikhail Lavrovsky or Vladimir Vasiliev as the hero and Maris Liepa as Crassus.

Sometimes an artist can not only redeem, but also completely alter, the balance of a work. Erik Bruhn's Don José, a remarkable performance, completely shifted the focus from Petit's Carmen to her victim. In Peter Darrell's *The Prisoners* Paula Hinton, one of the outstanding dance actresses of our time, was so powerful in the rôle of the wife that attention was concentrated upon her and one understood an unsympathetic character far better than the intended objects of one's sympathy, the prisoners themselves. Sometimes sheer physical allure can imprint a small rôle on the memory of the spectator for a lifetime: in the performance of Nicholas Orlov as the Drummer in the de Basil company's staging of *Graduation Ball*, good looks, panache, impeccable timing and an indefinable charm were perfectly combined. Occasionally a ballet may seem so ridiculous as to be beyond any redemption. A staging by Festival Ballet of *La Esmeralda* was about as unpromising an enterprise as we can remember, but when Tamara Toumanova arrived as guest artist in it – an atom-burst of temperament, style and beauty, with a bold cutting technique and her own ideas on costuming – she transformed the whole idiotic undertaking. She was both the life and the death of the party since after her departure it was impossible to view the ballet at all. Even a disaster as total as *Le Bal des Voleurs*, which lurched in and out of the Royal Ballet's repertory with considerable speed considering its crippling inadequacies of step, score and design, seems bearable in retrospect for one performance, that of Harry Haythorne, a dramatic dancer whom it would take more than this tissue of incomprehensibilities to obscure.

From classroom to stage

* A product of the Vaganova school from which all contemporary Russian training stems, Mme Volkova is one of the most celebrated dance teachers in the world.

Vera Volkova* pointed out in conversation with David Blair, 'Ballet is a science as well as an art because it has rules. It is a science, also, because if any of the rules which are propounded in the classroom are broken, not only the experts can see it is wrong but the audience too can see it is wrong. It is our job as teachers to see that the rules are maintained and that the dancers understand the rules. It is the job of the choreographer then to break all the rules, to use distortions from the basic classroom technique.'

This, in a nutshell, is what professional dancing is about, and even in the classroom, student dancers will comment enthusiastically upon classes given by professionals in which the breath of the theatre seems to touch their exercises. Every choreographer must use the classroom steps; they are his alphabet; indeed, they form the dictionary from which he will construct his choreographic sentences. But the straight classroom steps on stage have no theatrical impact. For the dedicated connoisseur there is always a great pleasure in seeing the academic vocabulary exquisitely performed – a pirouette can always be beautiful; entrechat six crisply beaten will delight the eye – but this is not the purpose of dance in the theatre, even in plotless ballets. Harald Lander's *Études* or Asaf Messerer's *School of Ballet* would be insupportable if we did not see the development of the dancer's art followed through from classroom exercises to their theatrical reality.

One of the chief contributions towards the theatricalization of the academic vocabulary is the roots that the choreographer gives a step in his score, and it is vital that in their training young dancers should understand early on the fundamental concept of moving with music – in the Soviet schools, for example, great importance is laid upon this interpretative aspect. Many choreographers find their initial lengthy study of a score suggests certain images which are then to be found in the bodies of the dancers who face them in the rehearsal rooms. The style of the music and the choreographer's own understanding of the bodies, will provide the starting point for the adaptation of classroom work that is to be transformed into a personal choreographic language. David Blair observes that many choreographers with whom he has worked:

> rely on well-trained classical dancers who come to them knowing instinctively the full academic vocabulary. From them the choreographer can take the vocabulary and adapt it – the classroom science is translated into art. Ashton, for example, does not have any steps ready but he is an absolute craftsman in that he has done his homework before he comes to rehearsal, he has researched into historical background, he has spent hours listening to the music and what he has prepared is the time that each part of his choreography is going

to take. He will always minimize rather than go on too long. But what he always brings to the studio is a pattern, a shape of what any dance or ensemble will take. There may be no idea about the basic steps, except perhaps the simplest idea that a particular piece of choreography will be terre à terre, will require pointe work, done fast and close to the ground. He then uses the dancers, looks at their bodies, asks for suggestions for particular steps, and he will take that and use it. He often choreographs absolutely in the classical idiom, then takes the straight classical bones out of it and introduces an element of surprise. You think a sequence will go on one way – he brings it back the other. You are always astonished by the choreography. My variation in the 'Elssler' pas de deux in *Fille* was done, I think, in about ten minutes. He'd got his pattern worked out; he knew that he wanted it to go from the O.P. corner to upstage prompt corner, and he wanted some sort of astonishing step. We tried all sorts of steps, first using different kinds of grand jeté en tournant or entrelacé to start with, and then he turned it in to a step which we call a revoltade in which you jump over one leg, and it still didn't have the element of surprise in it that he wanted, so we tried a single saut de basque in fourth and then we tried a

David Blair, who created the role of Colas in *La Fille mal Gardée*, retired from the stage – giving his final performance in this ballet – in the summer of 1973. The sequence has accordingly been illustrated by Nicholas Johnson of the Royal Ballet. The photographs were taken especially for this book by Anthony Crickmay.

The first step of the variation; from this the dancer goes in to the double saut de basque

On the way down out of the double saut de basque

Landing out of the jump above into fourth position 'absolutely out of the classroom'

double saut de basque landing in fourth absolutely out of the classroom, as it is taught; then, using the entrelacé idea, he said 'Let's see if we can't interlace the legs', and so then we came to the step where one leg crossed the other and moved into fourth position, and of course it threw me onto one side which he was absolutely delighted about and said, 'Now I want a relevé straight out of that' which brought me into a straight classical attitude. 'It doesn't look quite right,' he said, 'now put one hand on your shoulder and lift the other hand to the public.' That step was fine, and we did it three times. But how to get back to the centre? We tried chassé assemblé, double tour onto the knee. The music suggested a choreographic shape and I timed it to finish on the knee on the last note. But Sir Fred said 'No; bunch yourself up in to a tight ball and then EXPLODE.' So he did a bit of rubato, we stole from the phrase before, did the double tour on the quiet music and the exploding happened not on the expected double tour music but on the coming up out of my bunched position on the ground.

It seems to us invidious to detail the variety of ways in which a choreographer will adapt classroom training. One might as well consider the use of simple

'Now put one hand on your shoulder and lift the other hand to the public'

'Bunch yourself up in to a tight ball' – when the ballet was first made the dancer put both hands to the ground which was of course much easier but later it was changed to this position with the hands on the shoulders.

'and then EXPLODE!'

65

scale passages in a Mozart piano concerto. David Blair observes that 'What you might do three times in a classroom and then finish, Ashton will give a theatrical flavour by avoiding a "straight" rhythmic beat and seeking out a syncopation which is the element of surprise and personal flavour that marks the difference between classroom and stage.' Similarly the theatrical importance of épaulement cannot be too highly stressed since, by the subtlest adjustments of the position of the trunk, a perfectly straightforward and anonymous classroom step will be given theatrical life and flavour. In the beautiful sequence of pirouettes performed by the second male dancer in Ashton's *Symphonic Variations* the curve of the body and the rounded pose of the raised arm seem to spring naturally from a musical phrase.

Rarely if ever is a choreographer also a teacher. Since the nineteenth century there are but a handful of major creators who have maintained a continuing relationship with the classroom as teachers, though almost all are for ever keeping an eye on the development of talent in the school with which they may be associated. The supreme example of the choreographer as teacher, and more importantly as shaper of style, is August Bournonville, who, throughout his long career in Copenhagen, imposed a technical image as well as a choreographic identity upon succeeding generations of Danish dancers. At one time when he left Denmark he published a booklet, his *Études Chorégraphiques*, to make sure that his dancers maintained the purity of his teaching style. During his lifetime and following his death, a daily class was rigorously followed along the lines he had set out and it was maintained, embellished with enchaînements from his ballets, long after his death, and even today the Royal Danish ballet school preserves a set Bournonville class and have now put the actual *Wednesday Class* on stage as part of their repertory. For a fuller appreciation of this fascinating aspect of pedagogy we refer you to Erik Bruhn and Lillian Moore's *Bournonville and Ballet Technique* 1961. Bournonville's profoundly serious attitude to his training is testified by the copious notes which he preserved of his classes with Auguste Vestris, and these in turn formed both the basis of his own teaching method and also the material for the first scene of his ballet *Conservatoriet*, which is an affectionate evocation of a Vestris class at the Paris Opéra in the 1820s.

Other dancers of the nineteenth century, notably the Milanese virtuoso ballerinas, preserved carefully recorded classes from their teachers as their daily régime of practice, and in Peter Brinson and Peggy van Praagh's *The Choreographic Art* you will find the class that Pierina Legnani followed that had been set for her by her teacher Caterina Beretta. Similarly, the premier danseur André Eglevsky, when on tour, always carried with him the exercises given to him by his teacher Nicholas Legat, himself a pupil of Johansson.

There is inevitably the problem of those steps of virtuosity like the fouetté, which are nothing but sheer mechanical brilliance on the part of the dancer. They are often used, but rarely with any choreographic point. Pierina Legnani, queen of the fouetté in the nineteenth century, had acquired this trick in the Blasis school at Milan. When she went to Petersburg, as guest star with the Imperial Ballet, plainly it had to be used, and Petipa inserted a sequence of fouettés for her into his ballet *Cinderella* (just as he had used Henriette d'Or's weird talent for quintuple pirouettes on the right foot when he created a variation for her in *King Candaules*). Legnani's fouettés appealed to the circus taste of the Petersburg audience, and so, when Petipa came to write the third act of *Swan Lake* for her, he used them again, this time providing a perfectly valid dramatic framework since, with the repetition of these steps, the enchantress Odile is seen to dazzle the already bemused Siegfried. Fokine, who reacted strongly against the virtuoso element in Petipa's ballets, comments on the fouetté in his theorizing on the art of ballet which was published in Petrograd in 1916. Under the title *Delightful Nonsense* he observed:

If ballet forsakes its direct aim for expression the result is that one part expresses one thing, and the other the opposite. The most typical example is the fouetté. For me this is the most hateful invention of ballet. The dancer expresses ecstacy and joy, but her face – what does that express? Quite the opposite. She seeks for balance and the whole face proclaims it. The face betrays her fear of losing her balance. There are few who can watch the expression of her features while she moves; what a contradiction: unity of pose and movement is a law which, to my regret, is not felt by everybody. (C. Beaumont, *Mikhail Fokine and his ballets*, C. Beaumont, London, 1935, 1945.)

But fouettés have been given legitimate expressive power in ballets. The virtuosity of the 'baby ballerinas' of the early 1930s' Ballets Russes was legitimately exploited by Balanchine with the series of fouettés which brought to a close his poetic *Cotillon*; Massine made obvious use of them in the dance for the Top in *Jeux d'Enfants*. In Ashton's *Les Patineurs* the brilliance of the two most accomplished girl skaters is seen in their firework display of fouettés and pirouettes which captures exactly the effortless spins of professional skaters on ice. (There is no friction between the blade of the skate and the ice to slow them down hence the limitless spins of any good skater – curiously, skaters never 'spot' turns although this is imperative for dancers to preserve their balance.) John Cranko also uses fouettés with real dramatic point in the closing celebrations of *Pineapple Poll*, when Poll and her companions express their joy in a whirlwind of turns.

The development of lifts in pas de deux work during the past twenty years in the West owes much to the example offered by the Soviet Ballet. The almost acrobatic nature of double work in Russia can be traced to the experiments of the years immediately following the Revolution, when the very ingredients of ballet were called into question. In the ballets of Feodor Lopukhov (1886–1973) the language of classical ballet was extended by the introduction of acrobatic work, in part inspired by the physique of the ballerina Olga Mungalova who was capable of extraordinary acrobatic virtuosity and whose litheness encouraged Lopukhov to devise a new form of very high lift in double work. This example was absorbed into the instruction given by A. Y. Vaganova, the great teacher, whose system is the base of all Soviet dance training. At the same time she maintained that 'so-called theatricalized acrobatics or gymnastics, to be acceptable on the stage, should be based on the classical exercises.'

Once established, extravagant high lifts became one of the signatures of Soviet Ballet (gone are the days when the noblest of Petersburg ballerinas, Vera Trefilova, refused to perform the fish dives in *The Sleeping Beauty* third-act pas de deux because they were 'acrobatic' and therefore vulgar). They express both the new image of Soviet woman and also new aims of Soviet art: heroic, yea-saying, this is man, master of his own destiny and capable of performing any physical feats demanded of him. In some ballets the lifts are used with dramatic conviction, as in the duets in Yuri Grigorovitch's *The Stone Flower* and *Spartacus*. In 'concert' numbers acrobatic lifts are used unashamedly for 'firework' effect – thrillingly in *Spring Waters* and audaciously in the *Moskowski Waltz* in which Struchkova would hurl herself horizontally through the air at her partner Lapauri, perform a tour en l'air en route and be caught with absolute nonchalance with one of Lapauri's powerful arms. High lifts can be given poetic quality as in the one that has crept, via Russia, into Act II of *Giselle*, when Giselle is held in arabesque high in the air for a moment that seems the choreographic equivalent of a sigh. This we owe initially to Margaret Dale's 1959 television production of *Giselle* when Nadia Nerina was partnered by the Soviet star Nikolay Fadeyechev. What became known in Western ballet as 'Bolshoy

Nina Sorokina and Mikhail
Lavrovsky of the Bolshoy Ballet,
Moscow, in a typically spectacular lift

lifts' at this time (immediately following the Bolshoy Ballet's first Western visit – at Covent Garden 1956) are now commonplace. Similarly, the more demure and precisely placed line of a Western dancer's arabesque soon became extended upward and outward, following the example of Soviet dancers. On Soviet dancers these always look entirely authentic; they are the fruit of Vaganova's marvellous development of the classic dance. On Western dancers, where they have been appliquéd to a less exultant style, they can on occasion look mannered and artificial.

Plainly the classroom must reflect the artistic tastes and requirements of the ballet company it feeds. With New York City Ballet, the School of American Ballet produces dancers who must be attuned to the searching physical and musical demands of the Balanchine repertory. The Royal Ballet School in England owes much to the image of an English style created by the Ashton repertory. In former years, the Royal Danish Ballet School fed from the Bournonville repertory, and although today it owes much to the cosmopolitan image of the company itself, Bournonville classes are happily maintained.

Although the translation of academic steps to choreographic truth is hopefully in the hands of an experienced choreographer, there is a more difficult transfer of the dancer from schoolroom to company. The acquisition of technique, started in the school, will probably continue throughout the dancer's active life; the acquisition of artistry – that understanding of what the body is doing, that feeling for its expressive power – is only to be gained when an artist has been absorbed into a company. It is there that a sensitivity must be developed to the different requirements of various choreographies – Petipa cannot be danced like Ashton, nor Balanchine like Fokine. It is this awareness of artistic style, this feeling for the respective merits of the same steps in different clothing, that distinguishes good dancers and good companies. The 'company style' must have chameleon-like adaptability. In this instance we can justly claim that Britain's Royal Ballet dancers show exemplary skill, since in a season they can do more than honourably by such diverse works as Nijinska's *Les Noces*, Ashton's *Symphonic Variations* and *Enigma Variations*, *Swan Lake*, Robbins' *Dances at a Gathering*, Balanchine's *Serenade*, and MacMillan's *Anastasia*.

Music for ballet

James Agate was always a great believer in going to the ballet and sitting with eyes tight shut so that he could listen to the score. We sometimes feel that it is better to stop your ears and watch the dancing, for, of all musical forms, ballet scores are the most uneven in quality. The ballet audience can sit through the most deadly rum-ti-tummery of Pugni and Minkus and in the same evening be presented with scores by Stravinsky, Ravel and Debussy which are among the most important works of twentieth-century music.

In the nineteenth century the score was often no more than an anonymous accompaniment to dances. A few scores – and how few – stand out. Adam's work for *Giselle* still retains both a period charm and a dramatic vitality which it probably owes to the fact that he was working in close friendship with Jules Perrot and Carlotta Grisi; he said that the ballet had been devised in his drawing room. It is in the score of *Giselle* that we first find the use of *leitmotiv* to identify the principal characters. This was a change from the procedure common in the 1830s and 1840s of cannibalizing sections from well-known operas to provide the accompaniment for set pieces in some of the ballets: for example, the borrowing by Ferdinand Herold of Rossini's music from *Cenerentola* for the storm scene in *La Fille mal Gardée* and the tunes borrowed from Donizetti's *L'Elisir d'Amore* for the big pas de deux in Scene II. Adam was a marvellous exception from the common run of Bergmüller and Deldevez and their kind, who produced mediocre amiabilities by the yard.

It fell to Léo Delibes, at a time when French ballet was sinking into the decline from which it was not to recover for nearly seventy years, to show the possibility of ballet music. His first success came with *La Source*, 1866, when he was placed in tandem with Minkus – each writing two scenes of the ballet. In 1869 he wrote his most popular score, *Coppélia*, whose enchantment is undimmed even after one hundred years. Well made, vital and filled with dramatic colour, it has guaranteed the survival of the ballet, and it was this score and the subsequent *Sylvia*, 1876, which so delighted Tchaikovsky.

Tchaikovsky's introduction to ballet came in the mid-1870s when he was invited to write the score for *Swan Lake* for the Moscow Ballet. The fate of his score at this time is indicative of the parlous state of ballet music. The choreographer and conductor were both incapable of understanding the symphonic merits of Tchaikovsky's writing (the conductor declared that he had never seen 'so difficult' a score) and as a result it was unmercifully butchered, with cuts, deletions and insertions of gems from other composers to make it acceptable to dancers and audiences in Moscow.

In the 1880s the new and inspiring director of the Imperial Theatres, I. A. Vzevolozhsky, endeavoured to lure Tchaikovsky back to the ballet stage and he succeeded in 1888 when the score of *The Sleeping Beauty* was commissioned.

* See Appendix C.

The greatest achievement of ballet music in the nineteenth century was not immediately attractive to the Tsar, ultimate arbiter of taste, but it swiftly won its audience, and the ballet remains the pinnacle of attainment for the Imperial Russian Ballet. There is no need to insist upon its splendours, though the whole score of Tchaikovsky's third and final ballet *The Nutcracker*, 1892, would repay attention for despite its ludicrous scenario,* it has delicacy, precision and, especially in the first act, great charm. No choreographer has yet found a way of expressing both the magic and the undercurrents of melancholy and an almost feverish morbidity that can be discerned beneath its elegant surface.

The Tchaikovsky tradition was handsomely continued in Glazunov's compositions for Petipa, notably in the golden *Raymonda*, 1898, though here again an imbecile libretto does much to sabotage stagings. But it is to the Diaghilev years that we must look for the completely new understanding of what ballet music can do and, indeed, for the maturity of the medium.

A glance at the list of composers who contributed to Diaghilev's enterprise reveals a splendour of achievement not rivalled by any company before or since. Of the thirty-five composers whose music was used, no fewer than nineteen provided specially commissioned works. These include Stravinsky, Debussy, Ravel, Richard Strauss, de Falla, Satie, Prokofiev and Poulenc, and their compositions remain a staple both of the concert and the theatrical repertoire. These scores were composed in close collaboration with choreographer and designer. They were precisely tailored to the demands of the theatre and of a guiding intelligence – most often that of Diaghilev – and it is the unity of inspiration in works like *Les Biches*, *Prodigal Son*, *Petrushka*, *Le Tricorne* that, even at this distance in time, still seems so miraculous. Diaghilev sought the best in music and in conducting, as he did in everything connected with his company. His uncompromising standards are, alas, foreign to the majority of ballet companies today, where the mediocre and incompetent are all too readily accepted by public, critics and companies alike.

It was impossible to expect Diaghilev's standards when Diaghilev was gone. The Ballets Russes of the 1930s, that inherited much of the repertory and the Diaghilev audience, could not hope to imitate either Diaghilev's genius in discovering composers or his financial skill in sustaining such high-powered creativity. A remarkable experiment during the thirties was Leonide Massine's decision to use symphonic music for ballet. His realizations of Tchaikovsky's Fifth Symphony, Brahms' Fourth, Berlioz' *Symphonie Fantastique* (a more understandable undertaking since it has a positive dramatic structure), Beethoven's Seventh Symphony, Shostakovitch's First and Schubert's Great C Major Symphony caused a furore among music critics and dance lovers. In the event the experiment proved to be a dead end, although Balanchine and MacMillan among others have successfully made use of symphonic scores for their companies: Bizet's *Symphony in C* by Balanchine and *Symphony* (Shostakovitch 1) and *Song of the Earth* (Mahler) by MacMillan.

It is worth noting that the Diaghilev experience never affected Russia to any degree. The moribund Imperial Ballet had to be given a completely new identity after the Revolution; there was much urgent rethinking of the function of ballet in a socialist society and for some time it even seemed that ballet was doomed as an abominable survival from the Tsarist régime. Thanks however to the noble endeavours of the Commissar for the Arts, Anatol Lunasharsky, and the great teacher Agrippina Vaganova, the ballet was saved. Some of the old repertory could be preserved and this provided an example for new creativity. After the early twenties, when there was much experimentation, the creation of long narrative works, adjusted to the demands of a didactic aesthetic and the new identity of the theatre in Soviet Russia, continued. Composers such as Shostakovitch, Asafiev and Khachaturian, as well as many lesser known names, became involved in a quite exceptional output of big ballets. It produced three of the finest long scores of this century: Prokofiev's *Cinderella*, *Romeo and Juliet* and *The Stone Flower*.

Serge Vassilenko wrote about his composition for the three-act ballet *Mirandolina* (1946):

> Popular music had always interested me even before I took up composition. From my childhood when I was living in the country I used to listen eagerly to the songs of the peasants and I made myself write them down; but Russian folk lore was not the only one which interested me. During my many trips to Turkey, in Africa, in the Middle East, and in the countries of Europe, I used to listen to popular music and write it down. Italy attracted me the most with its marvellous climate and happy people. When I first went there I made it a rule never to stay in expensive hotels but to lodge in fishermen's huts or peasants' houses on the outskirts of cities. Thus I learned to understand the life of the working people and I used to listen to their songs. I made several visits to Italy and in March 1910 I was in Naples. Seated one evening on the terrace of a Trattoria I could see below me in a little square young men and girls dancing to the mandolin and castanets. 'How happy you are, you dance all the time,' I said to my waiter. He answered me by joining his two hands together. 'What happiness, Signor? It is our harsh suffering that you can see dancing and singing. It is fortunate that by paying for our songs and dances the tourists don't let us die of hunger.' I could not have imagined that thirty-eight years later the themes that I heard then would sing out again in my ballet *Mirandolina*, in the dance of the young girls in the first act and the farandole, the sorrentino and the tarantella of the last act. I also went to Calabria, where I transcribed the tunes of shepherds' songs which are found in the serenade in the second act. In 1946 the Arts Committee suggested I wrote a ballet on Goldoni's comedy *La Locandiera*: the Italian people would have to appear ardent and joyful; I sought to transcribe this vivacity and ardour throughout the whole length of the ballet.

The tradition of full-length ballets had lapsed in the West, but when she started her company in 1931, Ninette de Valois knew that it was essential to stage the greatest of the nineteenth-century classics to provide a foundation and education for her dancers and her audience. These 'classics' were mounted during the first eight years of the company's existence; their popularity was immense (how quickly public taste had changed in London since the débâcle of the Diaghilev *Sleeping Princess*) and there came the remarkable but inevitable challenge to produce British full-length ballets. Scores did not exist, so the Royal Ballet had to turn at first to Russia. In 1948 Frederick Ashton staged his version of Prokofiev's *Cinderella*. This was followed by *Sylvia*, *Romeo and Juliet* (for the Royal Danish Ballet), and then by *Ondine*, for which a score was commissioned from Hans Werner Henze. Ashton has noted on his collaboration with Henze, 'I spent several weeks writing the libretto and then I prepared for the composer Hans Werner Henze a detailed minutage of the music I wanted. I am more adamant than Carabosse on these occasions. Not only do I prescribe the amount of music I want, but also the *sort* of music. The danger, of course, in commissioning a score is that one tends to get too much music. It is much easier for a musician to sustain the interest of an audience than for a dancer to do so. The problem of continually delighting the eye by variations on the comparatively few movements of which the human body is capable is one which

Act III

Prelude + Vision   5´ min –
under water.
Pas. de. Supplication
Bert. + Hul. interrupted   2 min
y entrée + promenade of guests   1 min.
Grand Pas Classique   6½ mins.

    Adagio boys + girls   2 ⎫
    Var girls   1½ ⎬ =
    " Boys ".   1½ ⎪
    Coda general fast   1½ ⎭

Entrée of Kuhleborn   ¼
Followed y rush of Neopolitans   ½
Divertissement consists of 12 boys + 12 girls
+ 3 principal boys + 3 principal girls.

ie. All boys + all girls 1 min ⎫
into which enter soloists   ⎪
pas - de - six   1 ⎪
pasde - Trois⎱   1 ⎪
2 boys 1 girl⎰ ⎪
pas - de - Trois⎱   1 ⎪
2 girls one boy⎰ ⎪
12 girls + 12 boys   1 ⎬ 11 mins.
Var 3 girls   1 ⎪
Var 1 boy   1 ⎪
Var 2 girls   1 ⎪
All six to finish   1 ⎪
All 12 boys + 12 girls +   ⎱ 2 ⎪
all pas - de - six.   ⎰ ⎭

Solemn dance interrupted y Ondines
in frenzy - flight of Bertalda all
exit = pas - de - action   2 mins.
Pas - de - deux . O + U.   3 mins.
Apotheosis   1 min ?
                                                  ─────────────
                                                        32¼ mins
                              or better   30 mins.

Frederick Ashton's notes for his composer, Hans Werner Henze, on the minutage of the third act of *Ondine*, 1958

73

forever besets the choreographer. It is also difficult to explain to composers that dancers get tired and cannot keep on dancing nearly so long as an orchestra can keep on playing. I found the best method is to ask the composer for slightly less music than I want; as he automatically writes more we usually arrive at about the correct amount!'* * See Appendix F.

In his own version of the collaboration – *Undine: Tagebuch eines Balletts* – Henze tells how he came to work in London, composing during the day and visiting Ashton in the evening to play the results to him on the piano. Some details of the work were changed, but Henze's great concern was with the difficulty of composing a full-length score in a modern idiom that would be acceptable to the general public. When the score was completed an orchestral recording was made, and it was to this that rehearsals were conducted, since it had been realized early on that it would be difficult for dancers to work to the piano version. It is often found with the very complex orchestral sonorities of modern scores that a piano transcription is inadequate for rehearsal: themes that may seem clear in the orchestral texture are obscured in the piano reduction and the guidance that may be offered by one leading instrument in the orchestral web is missing from the keyboard realization.

In 1956 the first full-length British ballet score was composed by Benjamin Britten for John Cranko's *The Prince of the Pagodas*. The ballet was not a success – it has been suggested to us that Cranko, then only in his early thirties, was too much in awe of his august collaborator to ask for the cuts which might have tightened the dramatic action and made it more urgent – but the score has been unjustly neglected. It is an important Britten work, eminently danceable – Cranko did in fact create some extraordinarily beautiful if dramatically irrelevant dances – though saddled with an indecisive narrative.

A recent full-length score was created by the distinguished composer Thea Musgrave for Scottish Theatre Ballet in 1969. The ballet was the result of a very close collaboration between Colin Graham, who wrote the scenario and acted as the producer, Peter Darrell, the choreographer, and Miss Musgrave. Colin Graham and Peter Darrell had devised a very detailed scenario and once this had been completed they and Miss Musgrave set about planning and analysing the work. 'We all had a mammoth meeting. We sat down together and it took all night to work out the timing,' says Miss Musgrave. 'It was evident where the climaxes were and how the ballet was built. When I set down to writing to the precise minutage I was conscious of moments of repose – like an aria in an opera when the action is not particularly continuous but is expressive of feeling. But there are certain other arias when the action continues and the character develops which is not a "static" thing but a "becoming" thing, and I was conscious of using these moments to build up to whatever climax came. As well as going in smaller "chunks", therefore, the score moved in larger sections. In a large scale work you can't have short number after short number; you have to be conscious of an overall shape.'

Miss Musgrave did not come inexperienced to her task, for she had already composed an opera, and before approaching *Beauty and the Beast* she had made a thorough study of Petipa's manner of collaboration with Tchaikovsky.* She observes: * See Appendices B and C.

> I was conscious that *Beauty and the Beast* was something very
> different from an opera, and in a way harder. In an opera you can
> fall back on words and on recitative, which you can't do in a ballet.
> Strangely enough, there is much more music in a ballet and one is
> more conscious of dancers. Dancers have to dance and you have to
> have a rhythmical basis for things in a quite different way from
> singers. The librettist's problem, the dramatic problem, is that
> dancers can do certain things quickly which a singer might take a

long time to say; conversely, dancers may take a long time to express something a singer can say in a word or two. That has been worked out beforehand, but I became aware of another practical problem – the actual conducting. It is desperately important to get the *exact* tempo because dancers can't hold a leap in mid-air. This is a very real difficulty because with singers you can take liberties. Peter Darrell worked with the completed score. He had heard some work in progress – on the piano – and he is very musical, but even so he couldn't hear the orchestral sounds which are essential in their way. That is another problem with ballet. Dancers, let alone the choreographer, don't really hear what the score sounds like until the orchestral rehearsals, perhaps a week or less before the première. They don't know what to listen for, because the balances are different with a piano reduction. After the first performance it's easier, but I think this was a problem for Darrell, and he did alter some things when he had heard the score on the orchestra. Cuts are inevitable. We always expect them. When I composed the score I worked on a precise timing and I kept very strictly to it, but after the first performance – as with an opera – you find that certain things aren't quite in the proportion that you want, so you have to make some of what Norman del Mar calls 'invisible shrinks' – a cut here or there to make the garment fit properly – as well as one or two 'visible shrinks', slightly larger cuts, and when these were done the ballet benefited. It is very strange; when you work with an orchestral piece the form seems to take over, but when you put that on stage and you work in theatrical terms the theatre has its own demands. They may cut across the work in some way and you have to be aware of that, and work with it, because you are concerned with theatrical and dramatic timing. Some of the 'shrinks' can be so tiny you hardly notice them, but they make all the difference in tightening. A cut can just be a bar, but the section seems much shorter thereafter. We only cut about five minutes from the score yet it made the work much tauter.

I started composing at the beginning of the story and worked right through to the end. I was aware that there were to be repetitions, themes that increase or develop, and I always had my eyes on the final pas de deux. I knew that this was going to be something very special: I said to Darrell that I wanted it to be very quiet – not big and bombastic but close and intimate. So I reserved the strings alone for that, the only place they feature alone in the ballet. I knew I was working with a limited number of orchestral players and it is more difficult to write 80 minutes of music for a small number of players. You have to give the musicians a rest – they can't all play all the time – and you also have to give the audience's ears a rest and also save musical colour, reserve it for certain effects. The tapes which I used only came half way through because Colin Graham's libretto spoke of the Beast's 'wicked laughter' and I knew that it had to be stylized. I decided to use tape for a dramatic function. It had specific reason: for the magic realm of the Beast and for the time travel by the Beauty.

It is very curious to record that in another staging of this score the final pas de deux was left out, which ruined the shape of the ballet. It was also presented in one act. The result was that the ballet seemed much longer, because the proportions were wrong.

If a choreographer wanted to use one of my existing orchestral scores – say the Clarinet Concerto – I would be agreeable, but they

would run into problems with that piece because there is a certain freedom in it, in the sense that things don't always necessarily happen at the same time. This could be very exciting for a choreographer if he could give his dancers a similar freedom. The dancer could identify with the clarinet player and go with the player, so that the dance would follow the player, but it would not be the same on each occasion. I wouldn't cut an existing work. When you compose a full evening narrative work there are moments which are more spread out, and if they are tightened for some reason by cuts, it is not so important. But a work like the Clarinet Concerto is very carefully planned and is not cuttable. Any demand for cuts would mean that the choreographer could not think through an existing score and its problems, and I am not sympathetic to that.

An example of collaboration between composer and choreographer, involving not only commissioned music but also the use of some existing pieces, was the Matyas Seiber-Kenneth MacMillan staging of *The Invitation* in 1960.

Before starting the work, MacMillan had been strongly attracted to Seiber's music and felt he would be the ideal composer, and Seiber accepted the commission for his first ballet score. MacMillan drew up a detailed scenario that indicated precise running times for each piece of the action, together with full information about the characters and their emotional states. Seiber already had experience of writing music for films and was used to working to a libretto. During the period of composition MacMillan visited him often to discuss and amplify the outline. Only one fragment of the score was not specially written; Seiber offered MacMillan his *Pastorale and Burlesque* for flute and orchestra which it was decided to incorporate as the first entry for the young girl and some children.

Seiber worked through the scenario section by section, respecting all MacMillan's requirements. At the beginning of the collaboration, the choreographer had asked that, as far as was concomitant with Seiber's personal style, the score should be melodic – a request that owed something, probably, to the fact that MacMillan's choreography was becoming more lyrical, less brilliant and quirky. In treating this new theme, and in creating in a more directly expressive and emotional idiom, MacMillan needed the stimulus of melody as well as rhythmic variety. He also asked that a period atmosphere should be evoked for the social dances, which include a Polka and a Galop, and so Seiber produced the passage of the dancing lesson as pastiche Johann Strauss. MacMillan found the score for the most part very easy to work to; significantly, the most intractable passage proved to be the already written *Pastorale and Burlesque*, and, although for another reason, the percussive sections that Seiber and MacMillan had agreed on for some ensembles were not easy, because of the difficulty of expressing them on a piano in rehearsal.

MacMillan's method of work is to visualize movement only after he has been given the impetus of the music, hence the need, ideally, for the closest collaboration with the composer, particularly in a ballet, such as *The Invitation*, based on a set dramatic theme. At times Seiber would ask MacMillan to indicate the type of movement that he proposed to use and MacMillan would reply that until he heard the music he preferred not to create the movement!

Choreographers of course nurse musical ideas for some considerable length of time. Kenneth MacMillan had contemplated setting Mahler's *Das Lied von der Erde* for several years before he was able to stage it in Stuttgart, and Barry Moreland says, 'I have a reservoir of music in my head, things I've known for years, and about three months before I start working music seems to start to go round in my head which is relevant to the area in which I am going to work. In

Members of Scottish Theatre Ballet in the final divertissement from Peter Darrell's *Beauty and the Beast*, 1969, which had a specially commissioned score from Thea Musgrave

77

one instance, with *Kontakion*, I actually sat up the night before wondering what on earth I could use for music – I had been through months of searching and nothing seemed right. But the night before I had to go to rehearsal I was talking to someone and said "I must play you this Spanish mediaeval music. I'm sure you'll like it; I've had the record for ten years." And my guest said "What's wrong with that for the new piece?" And there it was.'

Sometimes a score will be changed during rehearsal. Paul Taylor has observed that when he started work on his *Orbs* he had a general idea of the piece and 'started with the Vivaldi *Seasons* which seemed obvious. But I got tired of the music quite soon and as I had always loved the last Beethoven Quartets they seemed to me just right and a lot more bearable.' The same thing happened with *Post Meridian*. Inevitably the change of score will imply choreographic adjustments. Taylor says, 'Whenever I change music it is a matter of going back and recounting and resetting the movement. Sometimes things sit perfectly well on the new music because we always have this instinct to be drawn to a musical rhythm.'

When Balanchine is about to produce a ballet he begins in one of two ways:

> Either I begin with the idea and then look for suitable music, or I hear a certain piece of music which inspires me with an idea . . .
>
> If I begin with an idea, I much prefer to have the music specially written for me and to be in constant contact with the composer

George Balanchine and Stravinsky at a rehearsal of *Agon*, New York, 1957

while he is writing it. I try to tell him exactly what I want, and together we conceive the general mood and we time some of the dance sequences. I have found that most ballet composers like to know when such and such occurs and how long it will last, whether a sequence is a dance sequence or a pas d'action and so forth. Like novelists, they are interested in structure first. In this way, they can start to compose at any point in the ballet and not at the beginning. Working on the story ballets *Prodigal Son* and *Orpheus* was a collaboration between the composers Prokofiev and Stravinsky and myself. (Balanchine, *Book of Ballets*, Doubleday, New York, 1954, 1968.)

For Norman Morrice the musical problem can prove slightly different, because of the demands upon his time as director of a company. Of his recent ballet *That is the Show* – one of his finest works – he said:

It is probably the work I was least ready to start, and enjoyed most. I have never worked so easily or so fast. I waited a year, because I liked the score so much I was terrified to begin: it always happens that the more you admire the thing that sets the ballet off, the more terrified you are to start in case you make a mess. I listened to the Berio *Sinfonia* a great deal – I had several months before I began work on it – and then I had two weeks' rehearsals in which I began to compose. Then we went on tour and I felt that this was hopeless because I couldn't complete the piece unless I worked in one sweep. So I left it, and then nine months later I began again when there was time for me to go straight through it. I worked very much from the text, which I found absolutely fascinating: for a long time I had wanted to explore the effect of a text which is not, or does not sound, particularly logical but which reveals certain pertinent aspects, all of which affected me very much. I found the structure of the third movement absolutely magnificent – it is wonderful that Berio could use all those symphonic fragments and make a fine piece of music – everything became transposed in to his own language.

The musical director

The influence which the musical director of a company can have is vast. It is to him that the choreographer may well turn to ask for ideas for a score or for guidance in choosing a composer for a specially commissioned score. In the broadest terms the musical standards of a company are his responsibility – the actual conducting and even the musical identity of the company will reflect his taste as well as that of its choreographer.

It is for instance impossible to overestimate the value of the work of Constant Lambert (1905–51), who was both conductor and artistic counsellor for the first twenty years of Britain's Royal Ballet. He found scores, reviving the forgotten delights of Auber and Meyerbeer; his own affection for Boyce, Purcell and Chabrier was reflected in ballets staged by the company; he was a consummate craftsman in arranging music for ballet (his Liszt orchestrations for *Dante Sonata* and *Apparitions* are models of skill*). His own compositions were of the greatest distinction – it may be said that he sacrificed much of his future as a composer through his unceasing labours for his company – and his conducting set standards which are still unrivalled in our experience of Western companies.

* For a detailed account of how a patchwork score is assembled see Appendix F.

Tribute must be paid to the musical standards which obtain in Soviet Russia. Yury Fayer's conducting for the Bolshoy Ballet was world renowned and it is impossible to say one has heard the inescapable *Swan Lake* until one has experienced the Bolshoy orchestra playing it with a love and passion that are testimony to a total identification with the ballet and Tchaikovsky's genius. The British ballerina Nadia Nerina was invited in 1960 to dance *Swan Lake* with the Bolshoy Ballet in Moscow. Certain adjustments were made in the choreographic text and Miss Nerina was asked to perform the Royal Ballet's version of the Act III pas de deux which was totally different from the Moscow version. Throughout all the rehearsals Yury Fayer was present, and because of his failing eyesight Miss Nerina in fact taught him the choreography at the same time as she taught it to her partner Nikolay Fadeyechev. Fayer learned all the steps as a dancer would, and the result was, as Miss Nerina records, 'absolutely superb. He could have taught the rôle to another ballerina.' It is this close understanding of the relationship between actual steps and phrases of choreography that marked Fayer's supremacy as a ballet conductor. It is a quality to be found only in the greatest practitioners of this very difficult art.

The New York City Ballet is a very special case in that its guiding genius George Balanchine comes from a musical family (both his father and brother being composers). His own musical gifts were trained in the Petrograd Conservatory and a unique musical understanding has marked everything in his career. This 'musicality' reaches its finest expression in the collaboration with Stravinsky's music, which dates from *Apollo*, and continues today. Balanchine observed many years ago that everything Stravinsky wrote could be choreographed, 'every note of it'. Proof of this could be seen in New York City Ballet's tremendous Stravinsky Festival in June 1972, which inspired Balanchine to create two fresh masterpieces *Violin Concerto* and *Duo Concertant*. In this context we might note Stravinsky's comment, 'I don't see how anyone can be a choreographer unless, like Balanchine, he is a musician first.' Stravinsky was particularly appreciative of Balanchine's musicality, which enabled him to free himself from a too literal approach to the music's structure and meant that he could make dance phrases that were subtly related to the score's phrasing yet had artistic independence.

Balanchine observes:

> A choreographer can't invent rhythms, he only reflects them in movement. The body is his medium and, unaided, the body will improvise for a short breath. But the organization of rhythm on a grand scale is a sustained process. It is a function of the musical mind. Planning rhythm is like planning a house, it needs a structural operation. As an organiser of rhythms, Stravinsky has been more subtle and various than any single creator in history. And since his rhythms are so clear, so exact, to extemporize with them is improper. There is no place for effects. Speaking for myself I can only say Stravinsky's music altogether satisfies me. It makes me comfortable. When I listen to a score by him I am moved – I don't like the word inspired – to try to make visible not only the rhythm, melody and harmony, but even the timbres of the instruments. No piece of music, no dance can in itself be abstract. You hear a physical sound humanly organized, performed by people. Or you see moving before you dancers of flesh and blood in a living relation to each other. What you hear and see is completely real . . . Stravinsky's effect on my own work has always been in the direction of control, of simplification and quietness . . . Stravinsky, as a collaborator, breaks down every task to essentials. He thinks first, and sometimes last, of time duration – how much is needed for the

introduction, the pas de deux, the variations, the coda. To have all the time in the world means nothing to him. 'When I know how long a piece must take, then it excites me.' ('Stravinsky in the Theatre', *Dance Index*, vol. VI, nos. 10, 11 and 12.)

Since 1958 the musical director of the New York City Ballet has been Robert Irving, formerly with the Royal Ballet. His work for the company is a complement to Balanchine's musical understanding, and has meant that the repertory and the dancers have been marked by an acute musical alertness.

The actual relationship between the dancers and the score to which they are dancing must also owe something to the contribution and guidance of the conductor. The conductor will often supervise the musical side of rehearsals, analysing and explaining difficulties to the dancers and helping them in the 'counts' that are so often used to fix rhythms and sequences of movement in the dancers' minds. With the new and often very complex electronic scores, as well as the demanding modern orchestral works that are used in ballet, tape-recording has often replaced the rehearsal pianist, but the musical director's analytic help is still needed.

It is a commonplace in appreciation of ballet that very strong differences exist in the musical understanding and musical style between, for example, the Bolshoy Ballet of Moscow, Britain's Royal Ballet, New York City Ballet and Maurice Béjart's Ballet du XXme Siècle. The Bolshoy's relationship to music owes much to the early training given to students, in which they are called upon to understand and work with whole sentences of music in the classroom. The result is a musicality different, broader in pulse than that seen with the Royal Ballet, which is always sensitive but less expansive and sometimes too politely efficient. The New York City Ballet dancers are concerned with remarkable speed and quickness of rhythmic response. They are called upon in the main to tackle more difficult scores and Balanchine's own extraordinary musical understanding marks his company's response to a score. Maurice Béjart's cavalier way with music, from Beethoven's *Ninth Symphony* to Ravel's *Bolero* by way of *Les Noces* and *Firebird*, not to mention Bach cantatas, reflects an unconcern with music as anything but an accompaniment for a series of pretentious messages to the younger generation. It is a nadir of musical realization.

The traditional interdependence of music and dance has undergone considerable questioning over the past twenty years. Ballets have been performed in silence – notable early examples of this were David Lichine's beautiful *La Création* and Jerome Robbins's *Moves*. The American avant-garde, centred on Merce Cunningham and his associates, has shown that chance noise, as well as silence, can be a potent contributor to dance. There is now developing what we may call the post-Cunningham generation, who reject the dance/music relationship entirely. Richard Alston typifies this attitude. He says:

> I listen to a lot of music and I love it, but I don't often work with it. Or rather I work with it 'in private' in that I get many ideas about time, rhythm and time structures from music; ideas can come from musical ideas. I found at one time if I used music that I really liked I ended up creating something that was very enjoyable to do, but the movement tended to be banal and very simple, getting into nothing but steps, running around on the beat. This is wrong if it becomes a habit and you happen not to be writing a piece about running. The point (perhaps the danger) for me with working with music is that it is not a habit, as it was with the previous generation where dance and music were inextricably linked. It was never made so when I started. I began working with ideas because body rhythms are different from musical rhythms. Someone once told

me that the timing of my pieces had 'conversational' rhythm rather than musical rhythm. Instead of having a regular musical shape my pieces had an asymetrical phrasing like speech. When I want to choreograph well to music I have to work slowly and I am usually quite a fast worker. Without music I work faster, because one can just think of movement, add on movement and branch off from what the dancers are doing: everything is dictated simply by what is there. You can structure the movement on speech rhythms.

Design for ballet

The decoration devised by Charles
Nicolas Cochin, the younger, for *La
Princess de Navarre*, 1745

From the very beginnings of ballet in the court entertainments of the fifteenth century, spectacular production was one of the chief concerns. The entertainments had to impress by their magnificence, and splendour was often the prime concern. During the Renaissance, an artist of the stature of Leonardo da Vinci was required to provide decoration; the Florentine intermezzi, the ballets de cour in France, the English masques, all used the finest artists of their time to help in the creation of beautiful theatrical illusion. In the eighteenth century the culmination can be seen in the works of the Bibiena family, and the decoration devised by Cochin the younger for the performance of *La Princesse de Navarre* in 1745 in the Riding School at Versailles suggests some of the opulence of eighteenth-century spectacle.

The Italian school of the Bibienas offered marvels of architectural perspective and this Italian tradition persisted in the constructions of Alessandra Sanquirico in the beginning of the nineteenth century – the apogee of neo-classic stage design. Romanticism brought a different requirement: an evocative naturalism marked such designs as Ciceri's for *Giselle*. This new tradition was to fall inevitably into rigid formulae of stage decoration, and laborious naturalism was commonplace with ballet design in Russia, where the Romantic ballet was developed by Marius Petipa into the massive spectaculars to which we have already referred.

It is from Russia, however, that the twentieth-century image of stage designing received its strongest impulses. In the 1890s Sava Mamontov, a rich Muscovite patron of the arts, had invited easel painters to provide settings for

Illustration of scenery by Sante Manelli, after Giovanni Galli, for *La Clemenza di Tito*, 1755, a typical example of the Italian school

Scene for *Maometta* 1822, by
L. Castellini after A. Sanquirico.
Coloured etching and aquatint,
c. 1827

his private opera performances and Mamontov's innovation was much admired by Diaghilev. During the decade from 1895 to 1905 Diaghilev had concerned himself largely with painting under the tutelage of Alexandre Benois and Léon Bakst, and it is their influence, as well as Diaghilev's own taste, which we see reflected in the decorative standards which were eventually to bring such renown to the Ballet Russe.

From the very beginning Diaghilev insisted upon close collaboration between designer and choreographer: he may have initially decided upon the partnership, but thereafter he required a very intimate communion between them. In the early years of the company Diaghilev made use of only Russian designers, and his first major departure from this came with the invitation to Picasso to design *Parade* in 1917. *Parade* is symptomatic of Diaghilev's constant interest in the newest artistic manifestations in Europe, and also of the working conditions which he inspired. Cocteau records, 'Those admirable months during which Satie, Picasso and I lovingly invented, sketched and gradually put together this little work, . . . a kind of telepathy inspired us simultaneously with a desire to collaborate.' (*Le Coq et l'Harlequin*, translated by Rollo Myers, Egoist Press, London 1921.)

The list of Diaghilev's design associates for his works in the 1920s is remarkable, including as it does nearly every major painter of the era. The repertory reflects the constantly changing identity and function of stage design, from the magnificence of *Le Pavillon d'Armide* and *Schéhérazade*, through the profound novelty of the Cubist ballet *Parade*, to the remarkable stage picture devised by Tchelitchev for *Ode*, in which light and receding lines of puppets were all employed to express the ballet's allegorical theme. New artistic movements (the Constructivist *Le Pas d'Acier*) and new materials (the use of talc and transparencies for *La Chatte*) all indicated the developing possibilities of stage design.

It is in the work of designers like Pavel Tchelitchev, Christian Bérard, Eugene Berman and Sophie Fedorovitch that we see the most rewarding continuation of the Diaghilev tradition of design. Bérard's first stage work was in 1930 for the ballet *La Nuit*, in a Cochran revue, and for the next twenty years his designs for ballet and the theatre reflect a high point of stage decoration. Henri Sauguet, composer of *La Nuit*, observed that Bérard delved into the music to stimulate his imagination, and this proved true in all his ballet designs. He worked for Balanchine in the 1932 Ballets Russes season and for Les Ballets 1933, creating ravishing designs for *Cotillon* and *Mozartiana*. Balanchine said of him on his death 'I have never worked with any artist who showed greater sensitivity in collaboration.' His designs for Massine's two symphonic works, *La Symphonie Fantastique* and *Seventh Symphony*, were an inestimable contribution to the success of these works. Bérard became an artistic godfather with Boris Kochno at the birth of the young French Ballet in 1945 in Paris, and his designs for *Les Forains*, a charming story of wandering theatre players, had a set which was erected in the presence of the audience. Boris Kochno analysed the work of Bérard as 'expressing in his serious and sad accents the underlying beauty of our time'.

Eugene Berman, who called Christian Bérard 'the most completely theatrical, resourceful and imaginative designer of his generation', contributed primarily to the revival of ballet design in the United States, where he worked for the

Jean Babilée and Leslie Caron in David Lichine's *La Rencontre* with designs by Christian Bérard as staged by Les Ballets des Champs Elysées in 1948

Ballet Russe de Monte Carlo, American Ballet Theatre and the New York City Ballet. In many of his designs we can observe a marvellous rethinking of ideas from the Italian masters of the eighteenth century, such as the Bibienas, among them *Devil's Holiday* for the Ballet Russe de Monte Carlo in 1939, *Concerto Barocco* for American Ballet Caravan, *Romeo and Juliet* for American Ballet Theatre, and *Pulcinella* for New York City Ballet – his last work. The American writer Allison Delarue observes in his *Dance Index* monograph on Berman 'How often Berman defines a shape or a gesture in painting, or balances weights as eloquently as does ballet.'

There is a very marked difference between the demands made upon a designer for a ballet company and a modern dance troupe (albeit the lines of demarcation between the academic dance and the modern dance are being swiftly eroded). Balanchine's rejection of design is usually justified by the riches of his choreographic inventions but the policy is inexcusable when it serves lesser creators. On the other hand too many companies rely on fusty nineteenth-century evocations. The more traditional presentation of a ballet company, especially one working in a nineteenth-century opera house, will require settings and costumes appropriate to their surroundings and their often conservative audience. A permanent set – more properly a permanent structure

Design by Eugene Berman for *Devil's Holiday* staged by the Ballet Russe de Monte Carlo in 1939. The choreography was by Frederick Ashton

— that is cleverly adapted, often replaces the nineteenth-century practice of painted scenery, as in the exciting designs of Nicholas Georgiadis for the Royal Ballet's *Romeo and Juliet* and Barry Kay's setting for *Anastasia*. Jean-Albert Cartier, director of the Ballet-Théâtre Contemporain from Angers, has made it part of his policy to commission designs from some of the most distinguished European artists in a healthy continuation of the Diaghilev tradition of involvement with contemporary art.

With costume design, historical and dramatic appositeness will always be flavoured by the personality of the designers and the artistic climate in which the work is being produced. An additional problem is the ability of the costume to move *with* the dancer, and for the dancer to be able to move *in* the costume. The weight of Bakst's opulent costumes for the 1921 *Sleeping Princess* is notorious; more recently in conversation with us Lynn Seymour said, 'Costumes are often a bind', while Antoinette Sibley said that it was not until after three or four performances that she could really dance in the long tutus designed by Lila de Nobili for the 1968 staging of *The Sleeping Beauty* at Covent Garden.

Among designers for British ballet Sophie Fedorovitch (1893–1953) held a special place. In a note written for a memorial volume, Frederick Ashton called her 'not only my dearest friend but also my greatest artistic collaborator and adviser . . . She was the ideal ballet designer. She not only brought a real individuality and vision of her own, of perfect taste and tact, which enriched one's choreographic conception, but she worked with one ardently throughout its creation; she always attended as many rehearsals as possible, and as she saw the choreography develop was capable of completely altering her conception to enhance the choreography and the dancers still more. She believed firmly

Nicholas Georgiadis' model showing his use of a permanent set for Kenneth MacMillan's production of *Romeo and Juliet* for the Royal Ballet in 1965

88

that nothing must hide the dancing or impede the dancers, and that the background should not distract; and yet, a *magic* must be induced . . . Her method of designing seemed to be a process of elimination, clearing the stage of all unnecessary and irrelevant details.' The couturière Matilda Etches, also writing of Fedorovitch, recalled the vital principle: 'No sooner would the costume be on the dancer when Sophie would say in her gruff voice "MOVE".'

It is to the modern dance company that we must turn for many of the most ingenious and forward looking design ideas. Because modern dance is rarely if ever narrative, the representational set and costume is avoided. The example of Martha Graham and her employment of Isamu Noguchi is one of the shining achievements in modern dance design, the possibilities opened up by Cunningham's dance ideas engage the attention of such avant-garde painters as Robert Rauschenberg, Jasper Johns and Andy Warhol. The Graham and Cunningham companies are most often seen in the context of a proscenium arch theatre. Many of the smaller companies, however, dance today on open stages and in the most improbable situations. The avant-garde's willingness to try anything, *with* anything, produces both stunning banalities and rare poetic insights.

Mercutio's death in Act II of MacMillan's *Romeo and Juliet* showing how the Georgiadis set is adapted. The model opposite is for the ballroom in Act I

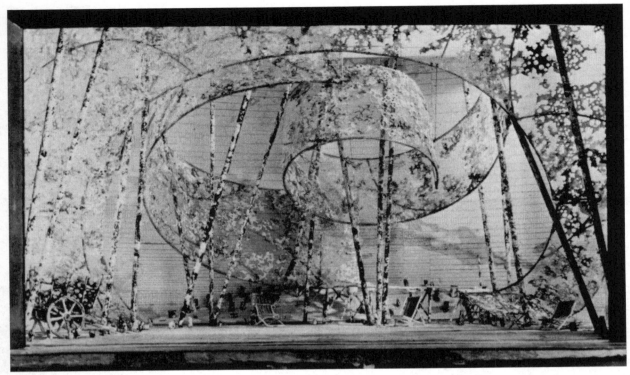

Model of the set by Barry Kay for
Act I of Kenneth MacMillan's
Anastasia for the Royal Ballet, 1971

Anastasia, Act I, in performance

Design by Lila de Nobili for Act II of *Ondine*. In Lila de Nobili Frederick Ashton found a worthy successor to Sophie Fedorovitch

Act II of *Ondine* in performance

Members of the Alwin Nikolais
Dance Theatre in *Scenario*

One of the greatest advances in twentieth-century design has been in the use of lighting (initiated by Jean Rosenthal for New York City Ballet and continued with the exceptional work of John B. Read in Britain) and the crediting of a lighting designer for many ballets is testimony to the importance of this ingredient of production. In its most ingenious application, with the Alwin Nikolais Dance Company, lighting can dominate even the choreography. Nikolais' spectacles are prodigiously complex studies in the effects of coloured light on bodies and, through his use of costuming, on the transformation of the dancer's shape. Nikolais is a magician who has sought to extend the potentialities of the human body, not through any development of movement technique, but by a brilliant use of costuming and accessories, as in *Mantis* and *Tent*, and in projections of coloured light patterns in many of his works, so that the dancers lose their identity and form part of a hallucinatory visual experience.

The designer speaks

In discussing the practicalities of designing for ballet, Kenneth Rowell, who has worked for both straight theatre, opera and ballet in Britain and Australia, says:

> It is necessary to work with the other collaborators right from the very beginning, whether it is a play, opera or ballet. So much hinges on the closeness of the collaboration. Any work in the theatre is a pooling of talents and this is crucial to the outcome: I think one must talk to the choreographer as soon as he starts planning his work. I feel that producer, designer, choreographer and director have to be chosen at the same time, and that is where the collaboration begins. You can go away and dream up ideas – you

Left Members of the Alwin Nikolais Dance Theatre in *Imago*, 1963. Both the picture and the one above show how dancers' shapes can be altered by Nikolais' very individual use of lighting and costumes

Right Members of the Sadler's Wells Theatre Ballet in Walter Gore's *Carte Blanche* with designs by Kenneth Rowell

learn this at art school in projects necessary to acquire technique –
but these ideas are rotten when you come to work professionally.

Sometimes a choreographer will have a very quick eye. Walter
Gore would come into my studio and see something – and he would
suddenly say 'I think we could use that'. This happened, I
remember, with *Light Fantastic*: I was putting down ideas about
the use of dolls, and this was a starting point for ideas in the ballet.

If choreographers have this developed visual sense it is sympathetic
and makes the designer's work much easier. Some choreographers
can be very sophisticated in their use of their own element but will
have no consistent visual sense. Balanchine has used marvellous
designers, but considering the bulk of his work, they are few and far
between. It was, for example, very difficult for me to design *Ballet
Imperial* for the Australian Ballet after knowing Berman's setting
for Britain's Royal Ballet which seems to me to be a classic piece of
stage design, absolutely definitive. But one also comes to feel that
there is not such a thing as a definitive setting; only for a certain
period is that true, when designs seem absolutely right for that
period. Time will show that tastes have changed and you have to
rethink the ballet. The aesthetic of periods changes; it also depends
whether a work is 'contemporary' when it is done, or classic in style.

When I designed the Australian Ballet's *Giselle*, my style of
painting could be integrated into the sets; now that I have found
myself as an abstract painter I find it much more difficult to bring
that aesthetic into *Sleeping Beauty* that I am working on now (1973).
The production has been three years coming to fruition, and in a
sense I'm glad it has, since I revised the designing twice. I have
tried to use the textures that belong to the period and suggest a
place. Because the stage is only thirty-six feet wide I have had to
make it very clean in its lines: I don't believe that you can use
masses of architectural detail on a stage on which you've got forty
dancers in elaborate costume (which are necessary). Since I wanted
the sets to be very simple – eloquent in the materials but not in the
details – I tried to make the costumes in line with that originally,
but it didn't work. I know that you can't get away from the tutu,
and I eventually decided that with *Sleeping Beauty* one can't get
away from the Baroque.

In a sense I tried to get away from the Baroque framework, and I
have made a compromise, I suppose, in that I have screens all round
the stage that turn from gold to a silvery green foliage like a formal
French garden. It is very spare, but the costumes are as fantastic as
I can make them (that is where I feel that the Bakst designs were so
magnificent). I have retained the Baroque silhouettes, but the
clothes are fantastic because *Sleeping Beauty* is a fantastic fairytale.
My solution to the difference of periods in the ballet – to make the
time change obvious – is to have the first acts a fantasticated High
Baroque and the last act a fantasticated Directoire style.

I can also make a bridge between what I feel and learn about
colour as a painter and my role as a designer, by decorating the
costumes with stripes and chevrons in colour.

What I love in working in the theatre – play, opera, ballet – is to
try and bring back the sense of colour. I find the theatre terribly
devoid of the brilliance and colour that Diaghilev and his
collaborators used. This is something I feel is lacking in good
modern design: the bare, metallic colours and shapes have become
a cliché. The best are very fine, but too much use is made of them,

Costume design by Kenneth Rowell for the Violet Fairy and her page in the Australian Ballet's production of *The Sleeping Beauty*, Sydney Opera House, 1973

and there is no element of surprise. I feel that the element of surprise in design is crucial to arousing an audience's interest and attention. This seems to have been drained out of the ballet and straight theatre, though less out of opera. Too much work in the theatre seems a cold exercise in pure design. I think this is a reaction against the excesses of the post-Diaghilev period. Directors in the theatre, and also choreographers, became scared of the audience's eye being filled with the stage pictures. Audiences are now being thrilled by colours again, and respond to it, after being fed a diet of austere stage pictures.

Although I find myself more frequently designing settings directly in model form – whereas I used to start with two-dimensional drawings or paintings and then translate them into models or even sometimes have the backdrops etc. copied from these designs – I nevertheless continue to find drawing and painting often the quickest means of conveying ideas to a producer. Model making – if done with care (and who wants to see bad models!) – is slow and laborious, but an idea can be sketched quickly and can give a convincing impression of a scenic idea. Sometimes, if one has a strong predeliction for using a particular material, it is more satisfactory to create some forms in a model using either the actual or simulated material. This may be particularly so if the texture of the material seems expressive and 'right'. Moreover, I have found that actually handling and working the fabric may provide the clue to the ideal forms it will take, and thus strongly influence the design.

There are of course no rules about the two different approaches and, more often than not, the solution is found in a combination of the two. That is to say, one may begin with a few sketchbook scribbles or visual notes (I hardly ever go out without a notebook in my pocket) which, when a pictorial idea begins to crystallize, can be referred to as you begin to experiment with forms in the model.

Model-making is very time-consuming, but I know that ideas can come from actually working with the model that would not actually have occurred to me were I not physically handling a material; for instance, the semi-permanent set I have made for the Australian *Sleeping Beauty*. I think that an audience is able to accept a semi-permanent set and not be bored with it (as we know from Shakespearian productions) if enough things happen to show the internal changes in the drama. I didn't think when I set out to do the *Beauty*, that we could any longer have, aesthetically or practically, interval scene changes, with wing changes, border changes and stage clothes being changed. Sir Robert Helpmann and Dame Peggy van Praagh agreed. Sir Robert is a true theatre man; you know that he is going to rely upon you as a designer since he has a very developed visual sense. His ballets have always had that special merit of strong design, from *Comus* and *Hamlet* onwards. It is wonderful to find a choreographer who will lean upon you; it is when they don't want too much, and want to take very little, that work is difficult.

The last scene of Kenneth MacMillan's *Le Baiser de la Fée* as staged by the Royal Ballet in 1960 with designs by Kenneth Rowell

Central to the whole problem of design, for all forms of theatre is to know *when* to stop giving. The impulse, for me at least, once I am into the work, is to do the whole thing in very visual terms; part of the technique is to know when to hold back and say 'That's enough', otherwise the thing will over-balance. The producer has the same problem; it's all a matter of light and shade.

I cherish my work with Kenneth MacMillan on *Le Baiser de la Fée* (1960) as one of the nicest and closest collaborations. We played the music a great deal at the beginning, and by the time we started work on it MacMillan had got across to me certain requirements: that the Fairy had to be hidden, that the Boy and the Fairy had also to move beyond time and space. *Baiser* was a designer's dream because the score is so gorgeous. I don't think one can work without being in sympathy with the music. MacMillan accepted everything I did, and was very encouraging to work with.

Sometimes I think that in the Diaghilev and immediately post-Diaghilev period, materials were better and lovelier. Today we have to be very careful with man-made materials – many of them I loathe – because they don't move. This doesn't matter with actors and opera singers so much, because you use them in a formal way, but the more ballets I do, the more I insist that the materials have something to do with the movement. Some man-made materials are useful, those with a glassy or synthetic look can be fine for a cloak; one must think of all fabrics as 'possible'. I always use a lot of paint

Margot Fonteyn as Ondine in the Shadow Dance in Act I of Frederick Ashton's *Ondine*. Lila de Nobili's costume was an essential aid to the characterization. Photograph taken during the filming of the ballet at Covent Garden. The film was directed by Paul Czinner for the Rank Organisation

on materials, it is a technique I like – to air-brush or break down fabrics, or apply patterns, or emphasize and bring out certain design elements in a fabric with paint. This avoids the 'raw' look of materials which seem as if they have just been bought and put on stage – they hit the eye too soon.

I learned a lot about ballet costumes from Martha Graham and the way she uses them. I think hers were integrated with the movement, and I believe she has lumps of material lying around the studio. When I was working with John Butler on *Sebastian* for the Australian Ballet, he wanted the dancers to wear big cloaks, so I had swatches of wool jersey for the dancers to rehearse in. It is ideal, though not always possible, to have the materials at hand to try on the dancers before the costumes actually get to the workroom and are cut, because then it is too late and too expensive to change them. Ideally it would be wonderful, if it were not too expensive and there were time, not to make any costumes until one had mock-ups and tried things in rehearsals. In making costumes I learned very early on, when I was making my first ballets with Walter Gore, that the choreographer had to be respected. Now I am fanatical about the dancer's ease of movement, because I think one has to respect their language. Just as you can't cover up an actor's mouth, you cannot impede a dancer's body. But, as a corollary, the dancer has to understand that if you do give him a shape it is to help his characterization.

Part of the problem is that dancers rehearse in their most comfortable clothes. That's a trap, and too often they don't see the costumes until the dress rehearsal. They are suddenly thrown into something that is strange and difficult to feel and get the feeling of. They ought to have them earlier. I know that the policies of theatres like the National Theatre, where they may have two or three weeks of dress rehearsals, are absolutely right.

I think any designer who imagines he can make a beautiful series of designs, and then hand them over to the workshop and go away, is out of his mind. It is also silly, because part of the delight is in seeing the designs gradually come together – and also being able to alter them. This is a very creative time, because fresh ideas may occur and, if the choreographer or director will allow it, you can make important changes and improvements. The people who are making the costumes will suggest shapes and ways of handling the material. A designer is unwise if he is in the hands of a good cutter and doesn't allow him to say 'if we cut this material on the cross instead of another way, look what it will do'. No designer can know all these things about costume making: it's a special craft and if you have got specialists, you must benefit from their experience and learn from their deep understanding both of the material and how it should be cut.

I think I must stress that one cannot do straight period reconstruction of an historical age: one must interpret it within the context of one's own style and one's own time. Certain pieces can be better served by having textbook reproductions of period costume, but I think they are very few and far between, especially in ballet. Even when a piece has got to look naturalistic, you must be selective in what you choose to stress in the period costume. Different periods see history in different ways. Victorians saw Shakespearian clothes one way, and now they look ludicrous to us because it was all to do with the Victorian aesthetic. You must select what you think are the meaningful lines and textures of the period; you accentuate. That's why the redesigning of the classics is necessary: a production speaks to one generation but not to the next.

A remarkably successful collaboration between a choreographer and a designer, who have both worked in classic ballet and modern dance companies, is that of Glen Tetley and Rouben Ter-Arutunian. For *Pierrot Lunaire* Tetley provided his designer with an initial idea of a vulnerable figure in a kind of cage, which resulted in a construction, both beautiful and totally right, which became Pierrot's world. Shortly afterwards the same collaboration was repeated, equally successfully, in *Ricercare*, staged first for American Ballet Theatre in New York in 1966. In an interview in *Dance and Dancers*, published in December 1967, Tetley said: 'I wanted two people who were so suspended in space, yet so separated, that they could not come together. I imagined a marvellous set, that was brass rods filling the entire space, with only enough room for these two people, and they could not go anywhere because of the intrusion of these brass rods. Rouben said, "that's a fantastic idea, but then you want it all to fly away in thirty seconds, and I don't know of any company that will put all that money into a set which has to disappear in thirty seconds". I began working in an old studio . . . in something called the Bohemian Hall where there happened to be two old portable foldable banquet tables. I grabbed these two tables, lowered the two ends and put them together, and it made a perch on either end for my two people. When they released from it they slid together and I became entranced with that idea. Rouben came to me and said, "I feel this thing should be in a circle". I said, "that's fantastic because today I started with something of the same image". So the shell or cone evolved.'

Jonathan Taylor and Sandra Craig of the Ballet Rambert in Glen Tetley's *Ricercare*, with designs by Rouben Ter-Arutunian

John Cranko rehearsing his *Brandenburg Concertos* with dancers of the Royal Ballet in 1965. Left, Vyvyan Lorrayne and right, Antoinette Sibley

In the happiest of collaborations between choreographer and designer there is often, as Norman Morrice has pointed out, an interaction of ideas that helps shape both choreography and design. An instance is the mutual inspiration that John Cranko and Elisabeth Dalton found in their work on *The Taming of the Shrew*, first produced in Stuttgart in 1969. Miss Dalton says:

> We talked a lot about how we were going to do *Shrew*. When it came to the actual designing, all Cranko asked for was space, and he added, 'and all the dancers want is nothing to wear, so go and watch what they like wearing most in class. You design it, and we'll discuss it.' Every day I went and watched the company doing class to see how their bodies worked, for it is terribly important to know

where you can put costumes and what has to be left free.

You can tell straight away what a dancer wants to hide by what they wear; leg warmers, or a scarf, etc., and this is a way you can hide certain things with accessories to the costumes. With the *Shrew* the main thing was to get the sets designed. This was done initially by paper cut-outs, with each dimension on a different piece of paper, because this was to be a permanent set. We wanted to get the Elizabethan feeling, like the Globe Theatre, with a centre feature and a bridge. The central unit could move forwards and backwards, but most important was the fact that Cranko wanted the scenes to change very quickly with no blackouts, so the set had to be cloths. I also had to try and change the shape of the stage, though with a permanent set this isn't really very possible. And I had to give the dancers as much space as possible. The next move was to have models made, and when Cranko and I had agreed on their suitability, I started on the costumes while Cranko set to work on the choreography. We had a very funny agreement whereby he allowed me to dress the dancers as I wished, provided he had not yet reached that point in the choreography. Cranko said 'I'll choreograph round what you design, but you must work in chronological order.' This was marvellous because each of us was watching the other very closely, and this is how a lot of the characters were built up.

Egon Madsen's role of Gremio came about because in the first scene, which was at night, the three suitors went courting to Bianca. I knew definitely they would be wearing large cloaks, so I went to the theatre wardrobe and found three of the largest cloaks there (from some opera or other) and told Cranko that they would have to wear cloaks like these. Madsen picked up his cloak, whirled it round, put it on and immediately started to sneeze. And Cranko said 'That's it! This man has forever got a cold; he is going to start with a cold at the beginning and it is going to get worse and worse. Everything about him is in his cold.' So throughout the whole ballet Gremio gets sicker and sicker and older and older. His solo, which is an impression of him singing when he goes to Bianca disguised as tutor, could show that he had a cold. His costume always had to have scarves. Egon Madsen looks very young, but Cranko wanted him to look old so I had to provide scarves and handkerchiefs to disguise his very handsome shape. Cranko wanted him to look an old fop, so we gave him a blond wig which was terribly, terribly curly with silly little hats on top, inspired by Cranach drawings. For the last scene he had another wig, which was completely straight, as if he had absolutely gone to pieces. What was amusing was the fact that he had so much dancing to do in the first scenes that his original curly wig actually did droop and come out of curl, without any help, as the lacquer melted. So, in fact, it helped to play the character.

I was working the whole time in the closest collaboration with Cranko. I don't think I put a single design on paper before consulting John and his agreeing it despite our fun race to get to the characters first.

There is a real problem in making sure both that clothes move well, and in ensuring that their colours remain true when they move. For example, anything blue tends to become too dominant when dancers start to move, while yellow shades tend to recede. All colour values change in movement.

One of the advantages of this very close collaboration between choreographer and designer is that the characters in the ballet become very clear to both creators, and every dramatic point can thus be brought out through the steps and the costumes. Even a minor character like one of the suitors in *Shrew* benefited: because Cranko saw the 'musician' of the trio is very neurotic and fidgety, Miss Dalton could match this in a costume that stressed the same point in decoration and detail.

Norman Morrice also stresses the rewards of collaboration: 'I used to think I couldn't bear decoration. Now I'm not so sure when there is harmony between the bodies and the surround or the scenery. I think there are no hard and fast rules: Nadine Baylis seems to me one of the most satisfying of all designers (we work together a lot) because she gets a simplicity which has nothing to do with simplicity for simplicity's sake. Basically, her designs must be part of the choreography and she can't begin to create until she has been in rehearsals and talked for ages. She is such an exciting person to employ because while the choreography is being made she really does add another aspect to the work. Without Nadine working at her very best the ballet would be less rich.'

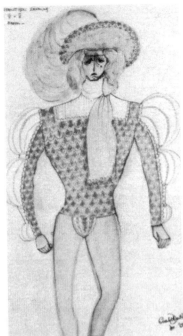

Costume designs by Elisabeth Dalton for Egon Madsen as Gremio in Act I and Act II of John Cranko's *The Taming of the Shrew* for the Stuttgart Ballet, 1968

Left Egon Madsen as Gremio in Act II of *The Taming of the Shrew*

The audience

'I'm not trying to do things that are original or great. I've never thought like that. What I am doing is entertainment – en–ter–tain–ment.' He lingers on the word for emphasis. 'I was brought up in the theatre – an Italian style theatre, with the philosophy that when the public pays money you have to entertain them.'
From 'Balanchine' a *New Yorker* profile by Bernard Taper, October 22 1973

We have thus far in this book attempted a study of the various elements that go to making a ballet, of their interrelationship and interdependence. It is the generosity of various creators with their time that has enabled us to detail their feelings and intentions. We have been, in fact, reporters rather more than critics, although when music, design, dance and choreography combine on stage we have to take up our critical function. And in the theatre – be it play, opera or ballet – it is only at the first performance that the merits or failings of a piece can be seen. The audience, far more than the critics, is ultimately the arbiter.

It is an extraordinary but undeniable fact that the joint efforts of choreographer, composer and designer will only be seen working together for the first time at the dress rehearsal. This state of affairs is dictated in nearly every theatre and opera house by the demands of repertory and performance and by finance. Incredible as it may seem, it is only at the first dress rehearsal that the dancers will be able to get the feel of the stage and scenery in their costumes; this may also be the first time at which they have heard the score 'live' since rehearsals will have taken place either with a piano reduction or with a tape of the score. Further, this dress rehearsal is profoundly unsettling for the artists: they have to adjust to design and music; effects achieved in the rehearsal studio may have to be rethought; with a dead auditorium, uncertain lighting and the inevitable interruptions, the whole piece will seem totally disjointed. This is obviously particularly true of a comedy work, where there is no response from that dead auditorium to tell the choreographer and his dancers where they will get the laughs.

Almost as artificial is the first night, at which the audience is a curious mixture of ballet lovers eager to see a new work, and those less happy souls who feel it their duty to attend for social rather than artistic reasons. Galas – especially Royal and State occasions – are usually deadly; the audience is there out of duty and applause is often thin and patronizing. Nevertheless, nothing can keep a smash hit down. The old Metropolitan Opera House in New York rose to its feet for Jerome Robbins' first ballet, *Fancy Free*, in 1944 and the Royal Opera House, Covent Garden, has never known a ballet première quite like that for Ashton's *La Fille mal Gardée*.

Sometimes a ballet needs to be 'nursed'. It may not have immediate audience appeal, but if a choreographer and his company have faith and if the critics lend their aid the audience may eventually appreciate the merits of an unusual or subtle work. How to encourage an audience to venture beyond the usual round of classic stagings is a major problem. It is a commonplace of ballet finance that with *Swan Lake* and *The Nutcracker* in the repertory, houses will always be good. Outside the capital cities, in particular, familiarity has always bred box office content.

Soirée de Ballet de Merce Cunningham

A Day or two is the title of this ballet.

The dance will be comprised of a number of separate dance events — solos, duets, trios, quintets and larger groups — sometimes seen as a single entity, and sometimes in multiple with several going on at once.

There are no predetermined characters and there is no prearranged story, so the characters of the dance become the characters of the individual dancers themselves, and the story is the continuity of the events as they succeed one another.

The dance is made separately from the music, and is not dependent on it. The three elements — the music, the dance and the décor — appear simultaneously, but independently of each other, particularly in the case of the dance and the music.

You as spectator can share this complexity of experience, but how you feel about what you see and hear is not determined by us. We present it, and allow each of you to receive this Day or two in your

But the decline in the number of suitable theatres in the regions of Great Britain and the crippling costs of touring large productions in both Britain and the United States has meant that ballet companies have had to try and solve two problems: to find repertories that will 'travel' and to extend public appreciation of what today's ballet is about. The Royal Ballet's New Group is trying to do this in classical ballet. The 'old' Ballet Rambert, which was crucified by the need to tour classic stagings in an attempt to secure an audience, was totally changed in 1966. It rose, phoenix-like, from disaster to become truly the Ballet Rambert once again with a brave new repertory and, within a few years, this experiment has proved itself. Rambert, with its new ballets and new style of dancing, has found a new audience and new theatres. The inclusion of theatres – very different in shape and function from the old touring houses – in universities and arts centres has also brought a different audience, younger and more ready for experiment. This new audience, in fact, would probably not be seen dead at *Swan Lake*.

This implies a polarization of audience taste. There exists in Britain one public eager for the new and another still convinced that the ballet is about Tchaikovsky and swan feathers. London Festival Ballet, while providing this latter diet, is trying to broaden the public's taste with contemporary works from Tudor and its own choreographers.

The British Arts Council's decision to encourage regionalism is a welcome step in breaking London's hegemony. For ten years Western Theatre Ballet laboured to win an audience, succeeded, and its translation in to Scottish Theatre Ballet, based on Glasgow, has proved that regionalism can work. The more recent efforts of Northern Dance Theatre to operate from Manchester merit encouragement. Nonetheless, there is a long way to go before the achievements of Munich, Hamburg or Stuttgart can be rivalled as world centres of opera and dance. (The Arts Council's total subvention to opera and ballet is below that spent by the city of Hamburg on its theatres.)

A word about international touring. It is a cliché that because ballet has no language barriers it is an international art and one immediately understandable in every country. Nothing could be further from the truth. National tastes in ballet are as individual and unyielding as national tastes in food. English ballet design is anathema to the French; conversely, French stage design has always been the envy of the English. What Eastern Europe thinks of as 'modern ballet' is both a question of artistic ideals and semantics since beyond the Iron Curtain a ballet is 'modern' if it deals with a modern subject though its language may be as dated as *Swan Lake*. Ballet in Eastern Europe is usually concerned with the presentation of an ideological theme, and the correct exposition of this becomes of paramount importance, as in the numerous productions of *Spartacus*.

It is this aesthetic gulf that makes it so hard for a Westerner to appreciate to the full the implications of much of the creativity in Eastern Europe. Conversely, the audience beyond the Iron Curtain – or, more accurately, the writers on ballet – will often consider Western ballet as either sterile or decadent.

Sadly, certainly companies which are highly regarded on their home ground can fail signally to win critical acclaim when they travel. The most remarkable example in recent years has been Maurice Béjart and his Ballet of the Twentieth Century. This company knows unprecedented success in Europe, playing to vast audiences in theatres, stadia, tents. Very much in tune with the young audience, who are suspicious of conventional ballet, Béjart's creativity defies (in every sense of the term) criticism. Uniformly slated in London and New York – where the brilliant American writer Arlene Croce put the matter precisely by referring to 'Beige Art' – he has played to packed and enthusiastic houses of young people who care not a damn for criticism but react with extraordinary eagerness to Béjart's visualizations of everything from Hindu mythology to Nijinsky's diaries.

Programme note by Merce Cunningham for his *Un Jour ou Deux* staged at the Paris Opéra in 1973

7- [PG] + [VH] - before JPG finishes
    [enlarge for entrances of DJ, LR et JJ]   [#3 avant tulle #7]

8- [WP]

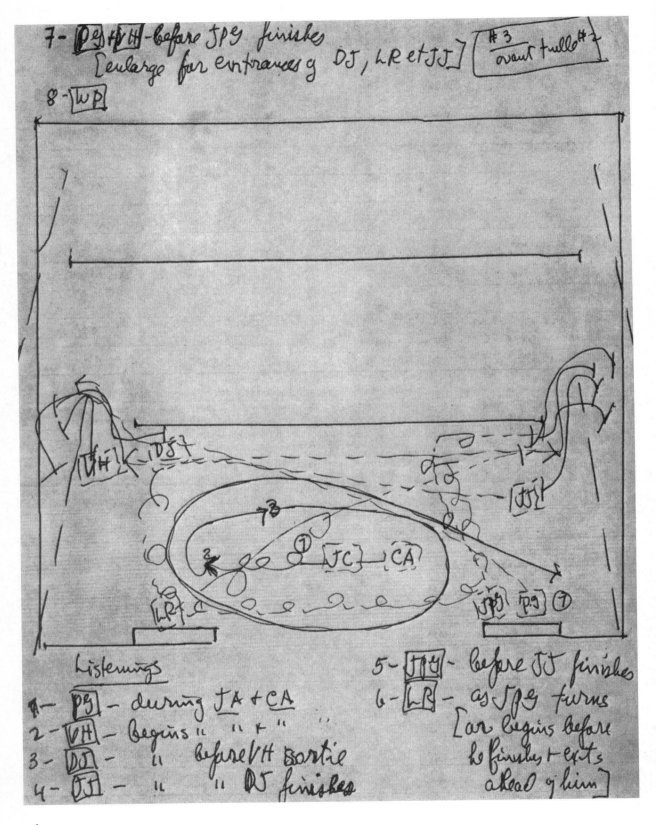

Listenings

1- [PG] - during JA + CA
2- [VH] - begins " " + "   "
3- [DJ] - "   before VH sortie
4- [DJ] - "   "   DJ finishes

5- [JPG] - before JJ finishes
6- [LR] - as JPG turns
    [or begins before
     he finishes + exits
     ahead of him]

Rehearsal picture showing the dancers of the Paris Opéra in the sequence sketched on the left

Choreographic note by Merce Cunningham for *Un Jour ou Deux*

On the other hand, many of our European colleagues have nothing but praise for Béjart and his works (he shared the 1974 Erasmus Prize with Dame Ninette de Valois!) and when the Royal Ballet visited Brussels – Béjart territory – for the Europalia celebrations in 1973 their reception was very different from that they have known in every other country. The Belgians evidently found Petipa, Ashton and MacMillan as unpalatable as the London critics do Béjart.

This question of national taste, of quite understandable national pride, and no less understandable prejudice, underlines the fact that ballet is an art of the theatre and it is the audience who must decide. Whether the audience will permit itself to travel with choreographers depends very much upon an open mind and an eagerness for the further development of ballet. Too conservative tastes are brakes upon the future of choreography – as they are upon all the arts. The future, therefore, lies as much with the audience as with the choreographer. Though tradition can never be rejected totally, it can not be used as a shelter from all the new ideals and ambitions of dance in the theatre. We can but urge the reader to be as venturesome as possible in seeking to understand dance in all its forms. As Merce Cunningham says: 'Come to the performance, and bring your faculties into action.'

APPENDIX A
Notation

Ballets are the most transitory of things – once a step has been danced it is dead. Until this century most ballets survived by direct transmission from dancer to dancer; where a play has a printed text and an opera a score, no form of notation was adequate to convey more than the merest skeleton of a dance. From earliest times of ballet history there have been attempts at notation but these proved ineffectual, and what we know of the nineteenth-century ballet and much of the early works of the twentieth century, has been due to the memories of choreographers and dancers. Some of the old ballets still performed are but unworthy shadows of their original selves and the loss of steps has been matched by an equal loss of style. The delicate inflections that give individuality and theatrical life can be lost after a few performances away from the choreographer's eagle eye. It is difficult to know how far to accept as true ballets that have been handed down over generations.

The caprices of dancers – eager to avoid a step that they dislike – the incessant attempts of producers to revive, rethink and renovate a popular old ballet, have all meant that the original texts of the standard nineteenth-century classics are largely lost. The most we can hope for is a reasonably honest approximation to what is hoped were the first intentions. The first productions of say *Swan Lake* and *The Sleeping Beauty* would now seem ponderous in the extreme, and the style of dancing, let alone the actual physique of the dancers, would probably strike us unfavourably. Nevertheless the present state of *The Sleeping Beauty* in Leningrad shows how continuity of performance and of training can preserve much of the atmosphere as well as much of the original choreography to marvellous effect.*

In the twentieth century there was initially little attempt to make use of the new medium of film to preserve either performance or ballet. How criminal it is that there is no record of Nijinsky, none of Karsavina, a bare two minutes of Spessivtseva, a few inadequate fragments of Pavlova, how disgraceful that even today far too few major interpretations and major ballets are preserved in this way. It is to two systems of notation, those created by Rudolf von Laban and Rudolf Benesh, that we owe the most serious efforts at the preservation of ballets by a written 'score'. Both systems have their advocates and nearly every major Western company now employs notators who record works as they are created and also write down the staple repertory. Furthermore, the development of video-tape now means that ballets can be filmed in rehearsal (and in performance) and these tapes serve not only as records but also as aids in rehearsal and guides to the dancers.

* The stagings by Nicholas Sergueyev of the 'classic' ballets for Britain's Royal (then Sadler's Wells) Ballet in the 1930s from his Stepanov-notated records were remarkably true to the versions which survived in Russia. When the Bolshoy Ballet brought their *Giselle* to the West in 1956 it was almost exactly the choreography we knew. When the Royal Ballet took its *Sleeping Beauty* to Leningrad in 1961 the Russians immediately recognized 'their' ballet as did we when their *Beauty* was shown in London. Sergueyev had been régisseur at the Maryinsky Theatre in Petersburg from 1904 to 1917 and when he left Russia after the Revolution he brought with him the note books which contained the Stepanov notation of the complete repertory which he had used in maintaining the stagings in Petersburg.

The Sleeping Beauty
La Belle au Bois Dormant

Marius Petipa's scenario. Translated from Petipa's original notes by Joan Lawson and first published in *The Dancing Times*, December 1942, January, February and March 1943.

This programme is to be found in a hand-sewn exercise book of MS. paper, of twelve pages. It contains the final notes and ballet-master's summing up, which he sent to Tchaikovsky. (The italicized sections are Petipa's instructions to Tchaikovsky.) The development of the action is written in Petipa's careful handwriting. The régisseur's plan is written in black ink and the musical illustrations in red. The appropriate paragraphs are written in the various inks, numbered similarly and joined together at the margins with red brackets. The first part of the Prologue is written in red ink and enclosed in special red brackets, which are absent elsewhere. Also in the margins are written additional remarks. The ballet-master signed the MS at the beginning and at the end, and at the top of the title page is written the date of the commencement of the transcription of the MS., 'July 10th, 1889'. After the title follows the remark, written in pencil: 'I finished writing it on July 5th, 1889.' The original programme was written in French.

Prologue

Scene I

The Christening of the Princess Aurora. A ceremonial Hall in the Castle of King Florestan XIV. To the right, a platform for the King, Queen and the Fairies – the godmothers of Princess Aurora. Centre stage back, the door to an anteroom. Courtiers, standing in groups wait the entrance of the King and Queen.

1 The Masters of Ceremony place everyone in their place, so that they may take part in the customary offering of congratulations and good wishes to the King, Queen and powerful Fairies, who have been invited to be godmothers at Princess Aurora's christening.
During the raising of the curtain a drawing-room march for the entrance of the lords and ladies.

2 Catalabutte, surrounded by court servants, verifies the list of Fairies to whom invitations have been sent. Everything has been accomplished according to the King's command. Everything is ready for the ceremony – the Court is assembled – the arrival of the Fairies is expected at any moment.
For Catalabutte's little scene, the march is made a little more serious, yet half-comic.

3 Fanfare. Entrance of the King and Queen, preceded by pages and attended by the governesses and nurses of Princess Aurora; these carry the Royal Baby's cradle.

Fanfare. Broad and very festive music. The King and Queen only just reach the platform and the cradle is set down as Catalabutte announces the arrival of the Fairies.

4 Entrance of the Fairies. The Fairies, Candide, Fleur de Farine, Violante, Canary and Breadcrumbs enter the hall first.

Graceful music 3/4. The King and Queen go to meet them and invite them to mount the platform.

5 Entrance of the Lilac Fairy – Aurora's principal godmother. She is surrounded by her own retinue of Fairies, who carry large fans, perfumes and hold the train of their Queen. At a sign from Catalabutte the pages run off and –

3/4 broadly.

6 Young girls enter with brocade cushions on which are lying presents intended by the Queen of the Fairies for her godchild. The arrivals form pretty groups as they present each gift to her, for whom they are intended.

3/4 rather animated and danceable. The pages and the young girls appear dancing.

7 The Fairies descend from the platform. Each in turn, they go to bless the child.

A little introduction for a Pas de Six.

Pas de Six

A Sweet Adagio. A little Allegro.

Variations –

    Candide

    Fleur de Farine *Flowing.*

    Kroshka Breadcrumb. *Which interweaves and twines?*

    Canary. *Who sings.*

    Violante. *2/4 animated. Plucked strings.*

    The Lilac Fairy. *A sweetly happy variation.*

    Coda. *3/4, fast and stirring.*

8 The Lilac Fairy, in her turn, wishes to go up to the cradle to give her gift to Aurora.

From 8–16 bars, when the Lilac Fairy wishes to go up to the cradle.

9 But at this moment a loud roar is heard in the ante-room. A Page runs in and tells Catalabutte that a new Fairy is arriving at the gate of the castle, one whom they had forgotten to invite to the ceremony. It is the Fairy Carabosse – the most powerful and wicked Fairy in the whole land. Catalabutte is horrified. How could he forget her; he is always so careful! Trembling he goes up to the King, to explain his shortcomings, his mistake! The King and Queen are upset. This forgetfulness of the First Lord Chamberlain will cause great unhappiness and affect the future of their dear child. Even the Fairies seem uncertain.

When the noise is heard* – very animated movement. [*Petipa repeats the words from the preceding paragraph in order to point out the position of the music more clearly. He marks these places throughout the entire programme in the same manner.]

10 Carabosse appears in a wheel-barrow, drawn by six rats. After her come some absurd pages – cripples. The King and Queen implore her to forgive Catalabutte's forgetfulness. They will punish him in whichever way the Fairy wishes. Catalabutte, breathless with fear, throws himself at the foot of the wicked Fairy, imploring her to have mercy on him, in return for his faithful service to the end of his days.
Fantastic music.

11 Carabosse laughs and amuses herself by tearing out handfuls of his hair and throwing it to the rats, who eat it up. Presently Catalabutte becomes completely bald.
She laughs and amuses herself by tearing out his hair – the music must fit the situation. The pages laugh spitefully.

12 'I am not Aurora's godmother,' says Carabosse, 'but nevertheless, I wish to bring her my gift.'
'I am not her godmother,' the music changes and becomes cajoling.

13 The good Fairies implore her not to spoil the happiness of the kind Queen and persuade her to pardon the Chamberlain's unintentional forgetfulness.
The music becomes tender when the Fairies persuade her to forgive the Chamberlain.

14 Carabosse only laughs at them – her mirth is echoed by her crippled pages and even by her rats. The good Fairies turn away from their sister with abhorrence.
Carabosse only laughs – a slight whistling.

15 'Aurora, thanks to the gifts of her godmothers,' says Carabosse, 'will be the most beautiful, the most charming, the wisest Princess in the world. I have not the power to take these qualities away from her. But so that her happiness will never be disturbed – see how kind I am – know that if ever she pricks her finger or hand, she will fall asleep and her sleep will be eternal.' (The King, Queen and entire Court are aghast.)
For this short speech – satirical, diabolical music.

16 Carabosse raises her wand over the cradle and pronounces her spell, then, overjoyed by her evil-doing and her triumph over her sisters, bursts out laughing. The raucous merriment of the monster is reflected by her retinue.
Pronounces her spell – a short, fantastic, grotesque dance for the crippled pages.

17 But the Lilac Fairy, who has still not given her gift to the child and who is hiding behind Aurora's cradle, appears from her hiding place. Carabosse looks at her with mistrust and anger. The good Fairy bows before the cradle. 'Yes, you will fall asleep, my little Aurora, as my sister Carabosse has willed,' says the Lilac Fairy, 'but not for ever. A day will come when a Prince will appear who, enraptured by your beauty, will plant a kiss on your forehead and you will wake from your long dream in order to become the beloved wife of this Prince and live in happiness and prosperity.'
The Lilac Fairy, who has still not given her gift – music tender and a little mocking.

18 The infuriated Carabosse sits down in her wheel-barrow and vanishes.
The good Fairies group themselves round the cradle, as if protecting
their godchild from their evil sister. (Tableau.)

*The infuriated Carabosse – energetic, satanical music. Group around the
cradle. (Tableau.)*

End of Prologue.

Act I
(Second Scene of the Ballet)

Four Suitors for the Princess Aurora. The Park of the Palace of Florestan
XIV. To the right of the audience, entrance to the castle*. The upper
storeys of the castle are hidden by leafy trees. A marble fountain in
seventeenth–century style stands at the back of the scene.

1 Aurora has now reached the age of twenty. Seeing that the Fairy
Carabosse's spell has not come true, Florestan is delighted.

*During the raising of the curtains, young girl- and boy-peasants, forming
groups, finish making large garlands of flowers, which they are making for
Aurora's birthday feast. Joyous music.*

2 Scene of the gossips.

Scene of the gossips and dance with their knitting – from 32–48 bars of 2/4.

3 Catalabutte, whose hair has never grown again, wearing an absurd wig,
exacts a penalty from some of the peasants, who have come into the castle
with needles and sewing.

*Entrance of Catalabutte. He is very happy at seeing the peasants. He
thanks them. The music changes – a fit of anger.*

4 He is forced to read them the order, forbidding the use of needles or pins
within a distance of 100 versts around the Royal residence. He orders them
to be thrown into prison under guard.

*He changes on seeing the old women embroidering with their needles. During
the reading of the order his anger grows and he orders them to be put into
prison.*

5 The King and Queen appear on the terrace of the castle. The four Princes,
suitors for Aurora's hand, accompany them. The Kings asks why the
peasants are being sent to prison. Catalabutte explains the reason for the
arrests and shows the evidence. The King and Queen are indignant. 'Let
them undergo punishment for their offence and never see daylight again.'

*The King, Queen and four Princes on the terrace. Characteristic and noble
music. Four beats for the questions and four beats for the answers, this is
to be pronounced four times. A broad 2/4, i.e.:*
Question: 'Where are you sending the women?' Four beats.
Answer: 'To prison.' Four beats.

Question: 'What have these peasant women done?' Four beats.
Catalabutte shows the evidence – four beats (from 32–48) altogether)

*The King's anger is now aroused. 'Let them be punished for their offence.'
Energetic music.*

112

6 The Princes, Charming, Arenant, Fleur-de-pois and Fortuné, implore the King that the guilty ones should be pardoned. Not one tear must be shed in the kingdom of Florestan on this very day, when Aurora reaches the age of twenty. The King allows himself to be mollified.

The Princes implore that the guilty ones be pardoned. For this request – 24 bars. The King allows himself to be mollified.

7 A general animated dance and a round dance for the peasants. To greet King Florestan and to greet the Princess Aurora.

General animation from 8–16 bars, in order to get to places. A melodious Valse (flowing – 150 bars). Corps de ballet.*

* Petipa's remark (written in pencil): 'Pas with hoops.' (New!)

8 The four Princes have never seen Princess Aurora, but they all possess medallions with portraits of the King's daughter. They all have an ardent desire to wed her and assure Florestan and the Queen of this desire. The King and Queen tell them that they will give their daughter complete freedom to make her own choice amongst them. He whom she loves will become heir to their Kingdom.

The four Princes have never seen the Princess Aurora. The music expresses a tender emotion and the ardent desire to wed her. Each individually expresses his love to the medallion with the portrait of the young Princess. Twenty-four bars.

9 Entrance of Aurora. She runs in accompanied by her friends, who carry bouquets and garlands. The four Princes are amazed by her beauty. Each one of them longs to be appreciated and loved by her. But Aurora dances with her lovers and shows no preference for any of them.

From 16–24 bars, which develops into another tempo. For Aurora's entrance – abruptly coquettish 3/4. Thirty-two bars. Finish with 16 bars, 6/8 forte.

10 Pas d'action.

Grand Adagio, very animated (mosso). The contest of the Princes. Occasionally the music expresses ardour, then Aurora's coquetry and later – broad and very noble music for the finale.

11 *Allegro for the friends – 48 bars, finishing with a Polka tempo for the pages.*

12 *Aurora's variation. Pizzicato for the violins, 'cellos and harps, or finally flutes and violins.*

13 *Coda. Vivace 2/4. Ninety-six bars.*

What happens during the adagio and pas d'action? The contest between the Princes. 'I am still so young,' answers Aurora, 'Let me enjoy my life and freedom.' – 'Do as you wish, but think what your kingdom demands, that you should be married and present your people with an heir to the throne. The spell of Carabosse has not ceased to haunt us!' – 'Calm yourself father, for the spell to come true I must prick my hand. I sing, dance, enjoy myself, but I never sew.'
The four Princes surround her and beg her to dance for them, as they have been told she is the most graceful dancer in the world.
Aurora, with her natural kindness, agrees to grant their request with pleasure. She dances, whilst her friends and the pages play on their lutes and violins. The four Princes in turn come up to her and pay her compliments and express their admiration. She redoubles her graceful and easy movement.

Not only the Princes and the Court are captivated by her, but all the townsfolk and villagers, young and old,* follow her changing aerial-like flights with curiosity. *General movement and dance.*

* Petipa's remark: 'It will be necessary to make groups of old men, women and little children.'

* An obscure remark in Petipa's text, which he included in double brackets and did not cross out.

14 Suddenly Aurora notices an old woman, who seems to be beating the time of her dance with her spindle. ((I have finished writing the programme))* The Princess seizes hold of the spindle, which she waves over her head like a sceptre, then she imitates the movements of the spinner. She enjoys the admiration expressed by her four suitors. But suddenly her dance is interrupted. She looks at her hand, it has been pricked by the spindle and is stained with blood. Terrified, her dance changes to a furious frenzy. She sways from side to side and finally falls senseless. The King and Queen rush to the side of their beloved daughter and, seeing the Princess's wounded hand, realize what dire unhappiness has befallen them. Then the old woman with the spindle throws off her mantle. Everyone recognizes the Fairy Carabosse, who laughs at the sorrow of Florestan and the Queen. The four Princes draw their swords and rush towards her in order to kill her. But Carabosse, with a diabolical laugh, disappears in a flurry of flame and smoke. The four Princes and their retinue run away in terror. At this moment the fountain in the centre-back of the stage is illuminated by a magical light – the Lilac Fairy appears in the streams of water.

Suddenly Aurora notices the old woman, who beats the time of her dance with her spindle – 2/4 which develops. It is beaten out all the time, into a 3/4 tempo, gay and very flowing. When the 3/4 begins, Aurora seizes the spindle, which she waves like a sceptre. She expresses her delight to everyone – 24 bars valse. But suddenly (pause – the pain – blood flows!) Eight bars, tempo 4/4 – broadly. Full of terror, now it is not a dance, it is a frenzy, as if she has been bitten by a tarantula. She turns and falls senseless. This will require from 24–32 bars. A few bars tremolo, with the sobbing and cries of pain, 'Father! Mother!' Then the old woman with the spindle throws off her disguise. At this moment the entire orchestra must play a chromatic scale. Everyone recognizes the Fairy Carabosse, who laughs at the sorrow of Florestan and the Queen. Short masculine-like music, culminating in a diabolical laughing tempo, when Carabosse disappears in a flurry of flame and smoke. The four Princes run away in terror. At this moment the fountain in the centre-stage is illuminated – here, tender fantastic and magical music. This passage must be long, as it has to last until the end of the Act.

15 'Take comfort,' she says to the weeping parents. 'She sleeps and will sleep for 100 years; but so that nothing can alter her happiness, you will sleep with her. Her awakening will be the awakening for you all. Go into the Palace, I will watch over you.' They place the Sleeping Princess on a litter and carry her inside, accompanied by the King and Queen and the first Courtiers. The noblemen, pages and sentries bow low as the procession passes. The Fairy waves her wand in the direction of the Palace. Everyone faces towards the door and on the staircase, suddenly stop. Everyone falls asleep, including the flowers and water. Ivy and creepers grow out of the earth, cover the castle and the sleeping people. The trees are thickly covered with lilac, whose magical growth has been commanded by the powers of the Fairy; the King's garden is turned into a dense forest. The Lilac Fairy's retinue surrounds her. She commands them to keep watch, so that no evil will disturb the peace of her godchild.

Tableau.

End of Act I.

Act II
Scene 3 of Ballet

Prince Desiré's Hunt. (1). A woody glade at the back of the stage, a broad river. The entire horizon is covered with thick trees. To the right of the audience is a rock, covered with plants. The sun's rays light up the landscape.

At the rise of the curtain the stage is empty. The hunters' horns are heard. It is Prince Desiré's huntsmen, pursuing wolves and lynx among the pine trees. The hunters and their ladies enter the scene, intending to rest and eat on the green grass. The Prince appears almost immediately with his tutor Gallifron and some noblemen from his father's Court. The Prince and his companions are served with food.

1 *The hunting horns are heard. The music of the hunt, which changes into the motif of rest – must be very short.*

2-3 In order to amuse the young Prince, the hunters and their ladies dance a round dance, throw javelins, practice archery and invent various amusements.

2-3 *The nobles of the King's court propose to play 'Blind Man's Buff' and other games. A quick 2/4 from 48–60 bars.*

During the games Gallifron urges his pupil to join in with his companions and particularly to become acquainted with the ladies, because he must select a bride from among the courtiers of his kingdom. All the kings, whose kingdoms are neighbouring to his own only possess sons. There is no Princess of the Royal blood whom he could select as his bride.

4 Gallifron, seizing the opportunity, compels the girls – the Royal courtiers – to pass before them.
Gallifron, seizing the opportunity, another motif.
16 bars before the dance begins.
About 24 bars for each dance of these ladies.

5 *24 bars. Dance of the Duchesses. Noble and proud.*

6 *24 bars. Dance of the Baronesses. Haughty and finicky.*

7 *24 bars. Dance of the Countesses. Coquettish and amusing.*

8 *24 bars. Dance of the playful Marquesses. They carry little darts, with which they tease the other ladies and their cavaliers.*

9 One of the Marquesses proposes to dance a Farandole, because some of the local peasants can dance it.

Farandole for Coda, from 48–64 bars, the heavy tempo of a Mazurka.

(Note for myself: Groups for 'Blind Man's Buff'. They play with the tutor. They push him with little arrows or darts. They can finish Pas de Bourrée, or a Farandole step with the peasants, who have come to present fruits to the Prince.)

All these girls try to fascinate the Prince, but Desiré, with a goblet in his hand, chuckles to himself over the fruitless efforts of these numerous beauties. His heart is still whole – he still has not met the girl of his dreams and he will never marry until he has found her.
All this is spoken during the dance.

10 Huntsmen enter to tell the company that they have surrounded a bear in his den. If the Prince wishes to kill it it needs a very accurate shot. But the Prince feels tired. 'Hunt without me,' he says to the noblemen. 'I wish to rest awhile in this very pleasant place.' The nobles and courtiers go off, but Gallifron, who has drunk more than one bottle of wine, falls asleep by the Prince's side.

> *Huntsmen enter to tell the company they have surrounded a bear. Quick 2/4, which stops quietly as they go out. 48 bars.*

11 Only as the hunt dies away, on the river appears a mother of pearl boat, adorned with gold and precious jewels. In it stands the Lilac Fairy, who is also Prince Desiré's godmother. The Prince bows before the good Fairy who graciously tells me to rise and asks him with whom he is in love.
'You are not in love with anyone?' she asks him.
'No,' answers the Prince. 'The noble ladies of my country cannot capture my heart and I prefer to remain single than marry a suitable Court lady.'
'If this is so,' answers the Fairy, 'I will show you your future bride, the most beautiful, the most charming and the wisest Princess in the whole world.'
'But where can I see her?'
'I will call her vision. See if she captivates your heart and if you will love her.'

> *Only as the hunt dies away, on the river appears the mother of pearl boat. Fantastic, poetical music. Grand music from 48–64 bars.*

12 The Lilac Fairy waves her wand over the rock, which opens and discloses Aurora, with her sleeping friends. At a new wave of the Fairy's wand Aurora awakens and runs on the stage with her friends. The rays of the setting sun bathe her in a rose-coloured light.

> *At a new wave of the Fairy's wand. Aurora awakens and runs on to the stage. A tender and happy adagio. A little coquettish adagio. Variation for Aurora and a small Coda. For the Coda the music must be muted 2/4 like in* A Midsummer Night's Dream.

12b All this occurs during Aurora's dance with her friends.

The enraptured Desiré follows behind this vision, which always eludes him. Her dance, now languid, now animated, entrances him more and more. He tries to catch her, but she escapes from his arms and appears again where he never expected to find her, among the swaying branches of the trees.
Finally he sees her in the opening of the rock, where she finally disappears. Overcome by his love, Desiré throws himself at his godmother's feet.

13 Where can I find this divine goddess that you have shown me? Lead me to her – I wish to see her, to press her to my heart.'

> *Where can I find this divine goddess that you have shown me? Very animated, passionate music – 48 bars, which must last until the Panorama.*

14 'Come,' says the Fairy, and places the Prince in the Boat which begins to move down the river as Gallifron continues to sleep.

Panorama

The boat moves. The duration of the music depends on the length of the Panorama.

14b The boat moves quickly. The horizon becomes more and more austere. The sun is setting. Night comes quickly. The path of the boat is starred with silver. A castle appears in the distance, which again disappears as the river twists and turns. But now, at last, here is the castle, the end of the journey.

End of the Panorama

The Prince and Fairy descend from the boat.

15 The Fairy, with a wave of her magic wand, opens the big doors. The ante-room is seen, in which the courtiers and pages are sleeping. Prince Desiré rushes onwards accompanied by the Fairy.
   The Fairy, with a wave of her magic wand, opens the big doors of the castle, 24 bars.

16 The scene is covered with a thick mist. Delicate music is heard.
   The scene is covered with a thick mist. Delicate music is heard.

Musical Entr'acte

Scene 4 of the Ballet

The Castle of The Sleeping Beauty

1 When the clouds and smoke disappear, the room appears in which the Princess Aurora is lying on a large bed under a canopy. King Florestan and the Queen are sitting in armchairs at their daughter's side. The court ladies, noblemen and pages, leaning against one another, are snoring noiselessly. Clouds of dust and spiders' webs cover the furniture and people. The lights are asleep. The flames of the fire are also sleeping. The scene is lighted in phosphorescent lights.
   When the clouds and smoke disappear. Mysterious music – 48 bars.

2 To the left of the bed, the door opens. Desiré and the Fairy enter the Sanctuary.
   To the left of the bed, the door opens. The mysterious music continues – 14 bars.

3 Desiré rushes up to the bed, but however much he calls the Princess, however much he shakes the King and Queen or Catalabutte, who sleeps on a stool at the Queen's feet – all is of no avail and he only raises clouds of dust. The Fairy remains an indifferent witness to Desiré's despair.
   Desiré rushes up to the bed. Excited music – 48 bars.

4 Finally he goes up to the Sleeping Beauty and kisses her on the brow. (Pause.)
   Finally he goes up to the Sleeping Beauty and kisses her on the brow – the music rises to a crescendo. Then a Pause.

5 The spell is broken. Aurora and the entire court awake. Dust and spiders' webs disappear, the lamps again light up the room, the fire burns in the hearth. Desiré begs the King to give him the hand of his daughter. 'What good fortune,' answers the King, and joins the hands of the young couple.

The spell is broken. The music expresses astonishment, wonder, happiness and joy. Everyone embraces at seeing each other again. Brilliantly warm music, lasting until the end.

Act III

Scene 5 of the Ballet

1 *March. Broad music – 48 bars.*
Divertissement.
Entrance of the ballet.
Like a festive procession of Louis XIV.

2 *Quadrille – Turkish; Quadrille – Ethiopian. Quadrille – African.*
Quadrille – American.
Procession of Fairy Tales.

3 *A grand dancing Polonaise from 80–96 bars needed for the procession of Fairy Tales.*

(1) Blue Beard and his wife. (2) Puss in Boots. (The Marquis of Carabas and his carriage with his lackey.) (3) Cinderella and Prince Fortuné. (4) Beauty and the Beast. (5) The Bluebird and Princess Florina. (6) The White Cat on a cushion of velvet and four tall lackeys. (7) Goldilocks and Prince Avenon. (8) The Golden Hind and Prince Charming. (9) Red Riding Hood and the Wolf. (10) Prince Coqueluche and Princess Aimée. (11) Tom Thumb and his brothers. (12) Giant and Giantess. (13) Fairy Carabosse in her wheelbarrow and her rats. (14) The Good Fairies from the Prologue. (15) The Lilac Fairy and her retinue. (16) Four Fairies, the Fairies Gold, Silver, Sapphire and Diamond.

The Prince and his Bride walk before the King. (Révérence.)

4 Pas de Quatre. The Fairies Gold, Silver, Sapphire and Diamond.
Allegro 6/8 fairly brilliant. 64 bars.
4 variations from 24–36 bars.

(a) Gold – a golden enchantress.

(b) Silver – it is important to hear silvery tones. *Polka tempo.*

(c) Sapphire – it is pentahedral. *Music in 5 time.*

(d) Diamond – brilliant, sparkling, like electricity. *Quick 2/4. A short Coda in the same brilliant character. 2/4. 48 bars.*

5 Character Dance – Puss in Boots and the White Cat. The miaowings, mutual caressings and pattings with their paws. For the finale, the scratching and shriekings of the cats. *At the beginning – amorous 3/4, but for the end 3/4 quickening miaowings. The whole dance must not be long.*

6 Classical Pas de Quatre. Cinderella and Prince Fortuné, the Bluebird and Princess Florina. *A short Andante. In the music is heard the song of the birds.*

Variation for Cinderella and Prince Fortuné – 32 bars – the tempo is full of passion. Variation for the Bluebird and Princess Florina 2/4. The singing of birds – 25 bars. A short finale of 64 bars. 'They kiss one another like doves.'

7 Red Riding Hood and the Wolf. Character Dance. Very short. She enters happily onto the stage with a jug of milk – *3/4, 32 bars*. She breaks the jug. She cries. The Wolf appears – she is frightened – trembles – the Wolf Pacifies her. *Polka tempo, a loving whining.* He fondles her, says he will forgive her, if she takes him with her to see her old grandmother. The dance finishes in Valse tempo, a little hurriedly. *She disappears, all trembling, attracted by the Wolf.*

8 Pas Beriçon. Character dance. Very short. Tom Thumb and his brothers. Seven persons appear, one behind the other, in one line, the first is very small and in the Giants' boots. They are happy because of this brilliant victory. *For entrance 2/4 – 16 bars.* They come in with big steps. *After these 16 bars, the 2/4 becomes very jolly.* The boys laugh loudly and dance round the boots. At the end of the dance the Giant is heard grumbling. Tom Thumb in a fright, puts on the boots, and the remaining six hold on to one another and run as fast as they can, pursued by the giant.

9 Classical Pas de Deux. Aurora and Desiré. *For entrance, brilliant music 6/8 – 32 bars. A fairly long and broad adagio with forte and in places with pauses. Variation for Desiré. 6/8 – 48 bars (forte).*
Variation for Aurora. This demands no connection with the preceding number. Coda 2/4 with great effects – from 80–96 bars.
General Coda – Character Sarabande. The music has big crescendos, exciting, overwhelmingly joyful.

Apotheosis. *Music accordingly. Broad, grandioso – motif of the song by Henri IV.*

Apollo, in the costume of Louis XIV, is lighted by the sun's rays and surrounded by Fairies.

THE END

The Nutcracker

Petipa's scenario is translated by Joan Lawson and reprinted from *The Nutcracker*, edited by Cyril Swinson (A. & C. Black, London 1960).

The version of the scenario which follows was written in French by Petipa. At the head of the first page he wrote: 'This is a copy of that which I sent to Tchaikovsky.' [Italicized sections are Petipa's indications to Tchaikovsky – M.C./C.C.]

Possibly Petipa made this copy hastily: it is carelessly written and sometimes he forgets to close a bracket.

In addition to Tchaikovsky's copy (which is preserved in the Tchaikovsky Museum at Klin), there is a third copy in the Moscow Conservatoire. The manuscript of the version which follows was preserved for many years in the Theatrical Museum, Leningrad, but was later transferred to Moscow.

For some reason the Mary of the story has become Clara, a name reserved in the original story for one of Mary's dolls. It was in fact Clara who was asked to give up her bed to the Nutcracker, and who later helped the Nutcracker in his battle with the mice, thereafter disappearing from the story.

The Nutcracker

At the rise of the curtain, the large dining room is lit by only one candelabra.

1 The President and his wife and guests decorate the tree.
    (Delicate, mysterious music 64 bars.)
9 o'clock strikes; at each chime of the clock, the owl on the top of it flaps its wings. Everything is ready and it is time to call the children.
    (All this takes place during the 64 bars.)

2 The fir tree is burning brightly, as if with magic.
    (Modulated music 8 bars.)

3 The door is thrown open.
    (Noisy and happy music for the children's entrance, 24 bars.)

4 The children stop, full of amazement and delight.
    (A few bars for the children. Tremolo.)

5 The President orders a March to be played.
    (March 64 bars.)
Each child receives a present.
All this takes place during the March.

6 *(Gallop for the children. 48 bars.)*

6b Entrance of the guests dressed very grandly.
16 bars for entrance. Then a Rococco dance. Tempo di Minuet. 'A good journey on the road to Du Mol.'

7 General amazement at the appearance of the Counsellor Drosselmeyer.
(At his entrance the clock strikes, the owl appears to flap his wings. The music becomes, by degrees, a little more frightening and even comic. A broad movement from 16 to 24 bars.)
The children, frightened, hide their heads in their parents' dresses. They are pacified, seeing that he brings some toys. Here the character of the music changes gradually.
(24 bars, the music becomes less dull, more clear and finally changes to joy.)

8 The President's two children nervously await the presentation of Drosselmeyer's presents.
(For this, No. 8, 8 bars of fairly grand music with pauses, in order for a cabbage to be shown and the same eight bars (repeated) for a pie, and the same pauses.)
'Pas with baskets.' (Drosselmeyer orders them to bring in two baskets, from one he takes a large head of cabbage, this is Clara's present – from the other a large pie – this is for Fritz. Seeing such uninteresting presents, the children and their parents seem disappointed.
(For this movement, only 4 bars, with a chord of astonishment – everyone exchanges glances.)

9 Drosselmeyer, smiling, commands them to place the two presents before him –
8 bars, motif of a Mazurka.
He winds them up –
another 8 bars Mazurka, during which the creakings of the key are heard.
The children are overjoyed, out of the cabbage appears a large doll and from the pie a soldier.
(Another 16 bars Mazurka for this little scene.)

10 Pas de Deux. (The clock is showing some time after 10 o'clock.
48 bars pizzicato with plucked strings of a good rhythmic valse.

* Petipa's remark: 'I'll have to make up my mind, I prefer the characters of Harlequin and Columbine.'

11 Drosselmeyer orders them to bring in two large boxes from which appear the 'Diable and Diablesse.'*.(Under these words is written 'Harlequin and Columbine.')
16 bars, in order to give an opportunity for a change to another Pas.
Demoniacal *Pas* of Dolls on elastic.
(2/4 fairly quick and syncopated – 48 bars.)

12 Clara and Fritz are now overjoyed, they thank Drosselmeyer and go to fetch the toys.
(16 bars of a happy, graceful andantino.)
The parents forbid them to play with such beautiful things.
(The andantino becomes more serious. 8 bars.)
Clara cries. Fritz is naughty. This occurs during the last 8 bars. In order to console them, the old Counsellor takes from his pocket a third present, the Nutcrackers, they can play with it as much as they like.
(Another 8 bars of a more animated Andantino.)

13 Clara is immediately enraptured with the toy.
   Now a polka tempo begins:
   Clara asks the Counsellor what the present is for. In the music one hears
   'Crack, crack' (under these words is written the 'knack, knack') all in the
   Polka motif. Fritz, hearing the 'Knack, knack' of the toy, becomes
   interested, and, in his turn, wants to crack a nut. Clara does not want to
   give the toy to him. The parents tell Clara that the Nutcracker does not
   belong to her alone. Clara gives her darling to her brother and sees with
   horror, that Fritz cracks two nuts with it. After this he pushes such a big nut
   into the Nutcracker's mouth, that its teeth are broken – 'Krack!' All this
   takes place during the 48 bars of the polka.

14 Fritz laughing, throws the Nutcracker away –
   8 bars of very animated music.
   Clara picks it up and with caresses, tries to console her pet.
   (Another 8 bars – less animated and more melodious.)
   She takes her doll from its bed and puts the Nutcracker in its place. This
   takes place during the 8 bars.

15 Lullaby.
   *16 bars for the Lullaby, which changes into a Fanfare of horns, trumpets and
   other brass instruments.*
   At this, Fritz and his friends tease Clara.
   Another 16 bars of Lullaby, and again the same noise in the instruments – 8 bars.

16 In order to stop this uproar, the President asks the guests to dance the
   'Gross Vater'.
   (8 bars before the dance begins.)

17 'Gross Vater.'

18 The guests thank the President and his wife and go out. The children are
   told to go to bed. Clara asks to be allowed to take the poor Nutcracker with
   her. Her parents refuse. She goes out sorrowfully, after she has wrapped her
   pet up.
   (Graceful March, finishing in a diminuendo. From 24 to 32 bars.)

19 An empty stage. The moon lights up the dining-room through the window.
   (This phrase is underlined twice and under it Petipa has written 'NO'.)
   (8 bars, mysterious and delicate music.)
   Clara, in her nightdress, quickly returns to look at her darling pet once
   again.
   (8 bars, even more mysterious for her entrance.)
   Something frightens her – *2 bars.* She trembles, she goes up to the
   Nutcracker's bed from where, it seems, a fantastic light is flickering.
   8 bars of fantastic and still more mysterious music.
   The clock strikes midnight.
   Pause in the music.
   Whilst the clock strikes midnight, she looks at the clock and sees with terror,
   that the owl has turned into Drosselmeyer, who looks at her with his sneering
   smile.
   After her fright a tremolo of terror.
   She wants to run away, but has not the strength. This occurs during the
   tremolo.

20 In the stillness of the night, she hears the mice scratching. She tries to gather strength to go away, but the mice appear on all sides.
Immediately after the tremolo – 4 bars, during which are heard, the scratching of the mice and another 4 bars for the squeakings.
Then – full of terror – she wants to take the poor Nutcracker and run away, but her fear is too great. She sinks down in a chair. Everything disappears.
(After the squeaking of the mice, another 8 bars of accelerated movement, finished in a chord.)
Just as she sinks into a chair:

21 The back door opens and the fir tree seems to grow enormous.
(48 bars of fantastic music with a grandiose crescendo.)

22 The sentinel on guard cries out: – 'Who goes there?' The mice do not answer.
2 bars for the cry and 2 bars for the silence.
The sentinel fires, *one or 2 bars.*
The dolls are frightened. *2 bars of fear.*
The sentinels will be like Hares – and are drummers –
8 bars to wake them up and 8 bars to beat the alarm, after this, 4 to 8 bars to form them into lines for battle.
The battle – *48 bars – 2/4.*
The mice are victorious,
(this is after 48 bars and the battle 8 bars),
and eat up the ginger-bread soldiers (sentinels.) Let there be an opportunity of hearing how the mice gnaw the ginger-bread.

23 The Mouse King appears and is welcomed by his warriors.
For his entrance gnawing, discontented music, grating on the ears, in which is heard 'couee, couee' (Hurrah). For the entrance of the King, 8 bars and 4 bars for the Hurrah (Couee, Couee).

24 The Nutcracker calls to his old guards. He commands – 'To arms.'
4 bars and 8 bars so that the troops can be set out in battle formation once again.

25 A second battle begins.
The 2/4 is continued.
A discharge of guns, the rattle of grape-shot, the firing and shrill cries are heard.
96 bars.

26 In order to protect the Nutcracker, Clara throws her shoe at the Mouse King. (Petipa's remark: – 'During the fight, the dolls come down off the fir-tree and begin plucking off the cotton-wool, and then Clara falls into a faint.)
2 bars for the shrill cry and 6 bars for the squeakings of the mice, who disappear. This happens at the end of the 96 bars.

27 The Nutcracker turns into a handsome Prince.
(1 or 2 chords.)
He rushes to assist Clara, who comes to herself.
Here some exciting music begins, changing into a poetic Andante and concluding in a majestic motif. (64 bars.)

Change of Scene. The Fir Forest in Winter.

28 Snow begins to fall. Suddenly a snow-storm occurs. Light white snow-flakes blow about (60 dancers).

They circle everlastingly to a 3/4 valse.

They form snow-balls, a snow-drift, but at a strong gust of wind, the drift breaks up and becomes a circle of dancers.

The End

The snow-flakes fall, larger and larger and are lit by electric light.

Tableau

For No. 28 and encircling Valse: during the 3/4 valse a strong gust of wind breaks the dancers into a circle.

Act II

(On a rough copy of the MS. in the margin, Petipa had written: 'This is what I sent to Mons. Tchaikovsky in Paris on March 9th, 1891, I have conquered all difficulties.')

(THE PALACE OF THE SUGAR-PLUM KINGDOM)
Very Fantastic Decor.

1 For the beginning of the Act before the rising of the curtain –

an overture which changes with the rising of the curtain to No. 2 and becomes more grandiose.

The back-drop and wings represent gold and silver palms – tinsel or tulle. In the background are fountains of lemonade, orangeade, almond milk and currant syrup.

2 *Andante quasi allegretto of 16 bars, which goes into No. 3.*

In the middle of these fountains, on a river of rose-coloured water, is seen a Pavilion of sugar-candy with transparent columns, where the Sugar-Plum Fairy and her retinue are seen.

At the rising of the curtain, caramels, marzipan, ginger-bread, cinnamon, nut-cakes, sugar-plums, barley-sugar, peppermints, lollipops, almonds, raisins, pistachios, almond cakes and little silver-coated soldiers (the Palace sentries), are found on the stage.

3 *The music becomes delicate and harmonious during a further 16 bars.*

In the middle of the stage, stands a little man in a costume of gold brocade.

4 Should I have arpeggios here?

The music broadens and swells, like a gathering storm. A quicker Andante until the end of this part from 24 to 36 bars.

The river of rose-coloured water begins to swell visibly and on its stormy surface appear Clara and the handsome Prince on a chariot of shells, studded with stones, glittering in the sun and accompanied by enormous golden dolphins with upraised heads. They ride above the pillars of the flashing rose-coloured streams of water, which descend and break into all colours of the rainbow. Six charming Moors, with sunshades hung with bells, in head-dresses made of golden shells and in costumes decorated with humming birds feathers, land and unfold an elegant carpet, which is all studded with peppermints, along which the Prince and his bride make their entrance. The

Sugar-Plum Fairy meets them. The silver-coated soldiers present arms. All the fantastic people make a deep bow. The little man in gold brocade, bows low before the Nutcracker crying: – 'Oh! dear Prince, at last you are here! Welcome to the Sugar-Plum Kingdom!'

5   *For this entrance, fairly stormy 3/4, 24 to 32 bars.*
Twelve little pages appear, carrying in their arms lighted aromatic herbs, like torches; their heads are like pearls. The bodies of six of them are made of rubies, the other six are made of emeralds, but in spite of this, they move gracefully on their two little shoes made of fine gold filigree work. Behind them follow four ladies of the height of dolls, but much more splendidly dressed and so richly decorated that Clara recognizes immediately they are the Princesses of the Sugar-Plum Kingdom. All four of them on seeing the Nutcracker, throw themselves round his neck with genuine sincerity and cry simultaneously, 'Oh! my Prince, Oh! my dear Prince, Oh! my brother, Oh! my dear brother.'

6   *8 bars of a broad and exciting 2/4, then 16 bars of martial music.*
The Nutcracker is deeply moved and taking Clara by the hand, he turns to the Princesses with emotion and says: 'My dear sisters, this is Mlle Clara Zilberhaus, I wish to present her to you. She saved my life; that is, if she had not thrown her shoe at the Mouse King at the very moment when I was losing the battle, then I should now be lying in my grave or, what is still worse, would have been eaten up by the Mouse King.'

7   *Here the broad 2/4 becomes quick and animated with joy at the freeing of the Nutcracker. 16 bars.*
'Oh! dear Mlle. Zilberhaus, Oh! noble saviour of our dear beloved Prince and brother.'

8   *Also 2/4. The trumpets of the little silver soldiers are heard. 8 bars and 8 bars in order to allow 'Chocolate' a moment of introduction for the dance.*
The Sugar-Plum Fairy makes a sign and on the stage, as if by magic, appears a table covered with jellies, etc: The little man commands 'Chocolate' to appear.

Divertissement

9 First Dance.
Chocolate.
Spanish Dance 3/4 from 64 to 80 bars.

10 Second Dance.
Coffee. Arabian, the Kingdom of Yemen. Coffee Mocha.
Eastern Dance from 24 to 32 bars of cloying and bewitching music.

11 Third Dance.
Tea.
Allegretto of the Chinese type, little bells, etc: 48 bars.

12 Fourth Dance.
Trepak, for the end of the dance, turning on the floor. (Obrouchky)
Quick 2/4 – 64 bars.

13 Fifth Dance.

Dance of the Flutes.
  Tempo Polka, 64 to 90 bars.
They dance, playing on little pipes made of reed, with bobbles on the ends.

14 Sixth Dance.

Dance of 32 Buffoons, with Mère Gigogne and her little children climbing out of her skirts at the head.
  64 bars, 2/4 accentuated rhythm, not fast, which combines with 48 bars, 3/4 for the entrance of Mère Gigogne and her children, jumping out of her skirt. Then 2/4 becoming much quicker, from 32 to 48 bars.
At the end a group with Mère Gigogne in the middle of the Buffoons.

A Grand Ballabile!

15 Seventh Dance.

Valse des Fleurs and with large garlands.
  8 bars for the start of the waltz, then, the same amount of bars as in the rural waltz in The Sleeping Beauty *(second scene).*
The little man claps his hands and 36 dancers and 36 danseuses appear, dressed like flowers who carry a large bouquet and present it to the Prince and his Bride. As soon as this is done, the dancers, as is usual in operas, take their positions and begin to dance.

16 Eighth Dance. *Pas de Deux.*

The Sugar-Plum Fairy and the handsome Prince.
  An Adagio with colossal effects, 48 bars. Variation for the cavalier, 6/8, 48 bars.
  Variation for the ballerina – plucked strings, 2/4, 32 bars, during which the water can be heard, splashing in the fountain. Then to finish 24 bars very accelerando. Coda another 88 bars – quick 2/4.

17 Ninth Dance.

A Grand General Coda for everyone on the stage including those who have already appeared in their dances.
  128 bars 3/4, very brilliant and ardent.

18 Tenth Dance.

Multicoloured fountains. Lighted fountains, etc.: etc:
  Grandiose Andante from 16 to 24 bars.

THE END

* (On the back of the MSS, Petipa wrote in pencil: '29 February, I have written this; it works very well.') (J'ai écrit cela; c'est très bon.)

126

APPENDIX D

The Creation of Les Noces

Bronislava Nijinska

The urge to pinpoint certain recollections takes me back in my thoughts to 1923, in the far-off period of the Ballet Russe of Sergei Pavlovitch Diaghilev, when I first made the acquaintance of Nathalie Goncharova, in connection with my work on the ballet *Les Noces*, composed by Igor Stravinsky.

The London season of the Ballet Russe, in which we were performing *The Sleeping Princess* at the Alhambra theatre, closed prematurely early in 1922. I had therefore left London for Paris to meet Diaghilev again over there.

When I saw him, I found him not at all as I had pictured him: expecting to find him overwhelmed by the abrupt end of the London season, I found him, on the contrary, cheerful, in high spirits, and delighted to see me again. Over lunch at Prunier's, Diaghilev talked of the coming spring season in Monte Carlo and of his plans for the subsequent season in Paris, where he intended to present a new ballet which he had long been meditating, on the story and to the music of Igor Stravinsky: *Les Noces* – 'Wedding'.

Talking about it, he told me how, in 1917, when they were all in Madrid, Vaslav Nijinsky and Leonide Massine had quarrelled furiously in his presence, each seeking to be the choreographer of this work.

'To prevent any conflict between them,' said Diaghilev, 'I decided to give this job neither to the one nor to the other. But I can tell you now how dearly I want to see *Les Noces* staged by you, Bronia.'

The plan to give Stravinsky's work in Paris, and the fact that the choreography was to be entrusted to me, filled me with pleasure. It was less than a year since I had left Soviet Russia. In Kiev, from 1917 to 1921, I had survived the Revolution, and, despite the bombardment of the town, machine-gunning in the streets, the destruction of buildings all round me, nineteen changes of government, I had contrived to work without interruption at the School of Choreography which I had started there, and which I called 'The School of Movement'.

I had renounced the theatre in order to dedicate myself to the development of a new kind of artist of the ballet. In this school, I had given a great deal of thought to my own choreographic potential, and had created, with my sixty pupils, a number of works. I felt myself bursting with new ideas, and burning to put them into practice. The moment that I had left Soviet Russia I joined the Ballet Russe in London, in 1921, after an interval of seven years since I had last worked with Diaghilev.

The Sleeping Princess, for which I was entrusted with the production and some of the dances, as well as dancing in it myself, seemed to me even then to belong to the long-ago. I was astounded that Diaghilev should have abandoned his innovations. I still breathed the air of Russia, of my 'School of Movement' at Kiev, of the harsh everyday atmosphere of the revolution, every aspect of which was vividly alive in me. So you can imagine my joy at being able to work on a new Russian ballet by Stravinsky, whose music had captivated me from my earliest youth.

After lunch, Diaghilev took me to the master to listen to his music. Igor Fedorovitch Stravinsky began by describing the action of *Les Noces*, which consisted of four scenes: at the home of the betrothed girl, at the home of her fiancé, the farewells to the girl, the celebration of the marriage.

Then he sat down at the piano and played through his new work. The music stunned me, took possession of my senses, set me pulsing to its rhythm. *Les Noces* seemed to me to be deeply dramatic, interspersed with occasional bursts of gaiety. These elements found their reflection in me, entering into my soul with the most profound and sincerely Russian of feelings; and, at that very moment, I saw clearly the whole picture of *Les Noces*, exactly as I would create the ballet choreographically.

Shortly after, we went with Diaghilev to Goncharova's studio. Nathalie Goncharova, whom I had never previously met, knowing her only through seeing reproductions of her settings for *Le Coq d'Or* and other drawings, the charming Nathalie Goncharova, so Russian in her looks, pleased me greatly. On a long work-bench, she set out the designs she had made for the costumes for *Les Noces*, all painted on large sheets of paper. There were about eighty designs, beautifully executed, in glorious colours, very theatrical and richly Russian. Males and females were both weighed down with heavy garments: very long dresses for the women, brushing the ground, and tall *kokoshniks* on their heads, the men all bearded, shod either in heavy boots or shoes with heels . . . to my mind, these designs would have been far more suitable for a Russian opera than for a ballet by Stravinsky.

How on earth could bodies, the instruments of dancers, enclosed in such costumes, shut in like violins in their cases, ever have managed to make any impression with their movement? Goncharova's designs seemed to me to be diametrically opposed to Stravinsky's music, and to the ideas I had already formed for its choreographic realization.

Once we had left Goncharova's, Sergei Pavlovitch turned to me: 'Well, Bronia! You were singularly silent, I trust the costumes for *Noces* delighted you?'

'In themselves,' I replied, 'these costumes are magnificent, and perfect for a Russian opera, but I find them "impossible" for a ballet, and especially for *Noces*; they have absolutely no connection with Stravinsky's music, as I understand it, nor for the choreography I envisage.' 'Be that as it may,' replied Diaghilev extremely coldly, 'both Stravinsky and I have approved Goncharova's designs. I think you had better not do *Noces*, Bronia.' 'Very well, Sergei Pavlovitch,' I replied, 'that is just what I was about to say to you, for with those costumes, I just couldn't create this ballet.' Diaghilev seemed very annoyed at my reply, and it was in that mood that we separated.

In the spring of 1922, first in Monte Carlo and then for the Paris season of the Ballet Russe, I did the choreography for *Le Renard*, by Stravinsky, with scenery and costumes designed by Michael Larionov.

For a whole year, neither Diaghilev nor Stravinsky brought up the question of *Noces* with me again. Not until the spring of 1923 did Diaghilev say to me. 'Bronia, I have finally decided to give *Noces* in Paris next May. (We were sitting in my little drawing-room.) Are you prepared to start rehearsals and make this ballet? How do you see it? You remember the first scene? We are in the home of the bride-to-be. She is sitting in a great Russian armchair, at the side of the stage, and her friends are combing her hair and braiding it into plaits . . .' 'No,' I broke in, 'there shouldn't be an armchair, nor a comb, much less hair!' I seized a pen and a sheet of paper, and immediately drew the girl with many plaits, three metres in length. Her friends holding the plaits, formed a group

around her. Diaghilev burst out laughing – often a sign of satisfaction with him.

'And what happens next? How are the young girls to comb such very long tresses?' he enquired. 'They are not going to comb them,' I replied, 'their dance, on point, and the bride's dance will express the rhythm of plaiting.'

As I went on drawing, I explained my idea of the choreography and of the setting. Diaghilev seemed more and more amused. 'A Russian ballet danced on point!' he exclaimed. Boris Kochno, who was with him, listened with great attention. Once again, I told Diaghilev of my rejection of Goncharova's conception of settings and costumes. 'What she designed was in the extravagant and brilliant style of one of the old operas about Boyars, but not that of a peasant wedding. I would like the very simplest of costumes, and all the same for everyone.'

Diaghilev agreed. 'You start work as you wish on *Les Noces*, and when the choreography is finished, Goncharova and I will come to see it, and she shall make completely new designs. But start rehearsing quickly,' and I did.

The action of *Les Noces* takes place in a peasant family. Such nuptials, in ancient Russia, had always seemed to me to have an element of drama; drama, in that chance decided the lot of the engaged couple who had been chosen by their parents to whom they were bound in obedience. No question of love entered into it. The young girl could know nothing whatsoever of the family she was about to join, and of the future that awaited her; would she be loved by her husband? would she be made welcome as a member of that unknown family? Not only would she be forced to submit to her husband, but also to his parents. It could be that, loved and cherished by her own family, she might be turned into no better than a drudge, an extra pair of hands, in another, new and uncouth family. The spirit of the innocent girl is anxious, deeply troubled, for she is about to leave for ever the carefree life of the beloved daughter of a devoted mother.

For his part, the young man has no idea either as to how life will be for him, with a young girl whom he knows not at all, or very little. How can it be possible

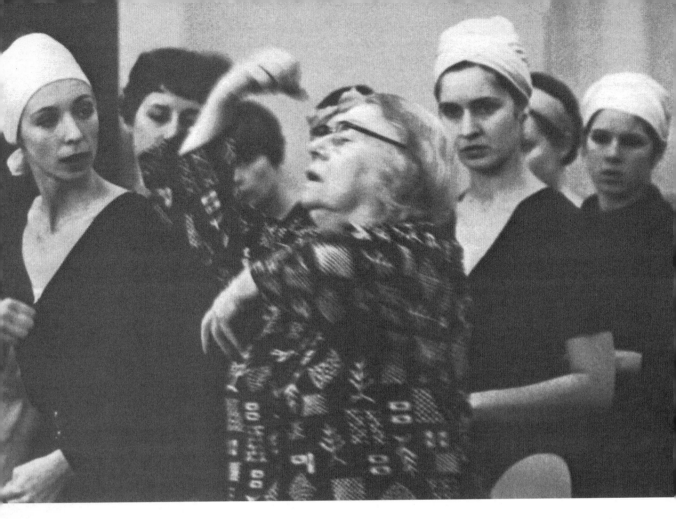

Bronislava Nijinska rehearsing
members of the Royal Ballet in *Les
Noces*

for two such creatures to feel rejoicing during the ceremonies attending their
marriage? Both are deep in other thoughts. Only the parents and friends are
happy, for to them a wedding is a matter of festivities, of feasting, of singing, or
bucolic dancing. The feelings of the newly-weds are far removed from all that,
as they try to reach mutual understanding in their souls and hearts when they
are united in wedlock.

It was from such a conception of a peasant wedding, from such sentiments,
that the ideas for the choreography were born. It was with this vision of *Les
Noces* that I approached the staging: to present, to bring to life in a ballet, the
rituals and the reality of such nuptials seemed to me to require an approach to
theatre different from my own form of theatre in which pure movement is given
form and expression. Mime was foreign to me, props useless.

Stravinsky's own libretto was all I needed, and everything came to me from
the inspiring music which, passing through me, transformed itself into movement, into the whole action of the ballet.

His own rhythm, the deep, heavy atmosphere with such rare flashes of gaiety,
themselves engendered the choreographic shape. And in this very fact lay the
idea of the possibility which showed itself to me, a fresh path: to lift the so-
called corps de ballet to a higher artistic level, in which the whole action would
be expressed. Not one single dancer standing out from the others, no soloists.
In this way, everyone would be moulded together in one throughout the
movement.

130

Drawing by Natalia Goncharova for *Les Noces*, 1923

In my conception, the entire company of dancers, just as the whole orchestra, would speak as one to indicate the shades of meaning of the choreography. The action of the individuals would not be explained by themselves *as* individuals, but by the whole. The betrothed girl and her friends would be bound together by a common expression of the whole action; while the young friends of the groom, lads enjoying themselves before a wedding, would only form a single unit with him. The parents of both sides would figure only as secondary characters, virtually blanks.

In the fourth scene all action would have ceased and only the dance would demonstrate the 'authority' of the ensemble.

The female side was to be led by Lubov Tchernicheva, who, with her technique, would embody and involve the whole matter, performing at moments a few solo steps as required by the music. Similarly, the masculine bloc would be led by one of the leading dancers of the company, the excellent Leon Woizikowski.

Whilst I was engaged in working out the first two scenes of the ballet, Igor Stravinsky was not in Monte Carlo. He arrived a bit later, to help me and also the pianist to find our way about the very complicated fourth section, and explain it to us. This work on the music with Igor Stravinsky himself left on me for ever the marks of his powerful imprint.

When the choreography of *Noces* was all but complete, there remained unfinished only one small part of the fourth tableau.

Natalia Goncharova and Michael Larionov arrived at Diaghilev's behest to spend three days in Monte Carlo, to see my choreography, discuss it with me, and then to make fresh designs for both costumes and décors.

I explained my ideas to Goncharova, pointing out to her the necessity of having very simple Russian costumes, in one colour only. This was essential in order to maintain the integrity of the choreography. I was very definite about the need to avoid heavy footwear and heels, and to have only plain dance shoes as Diaghilev and I had already agreed.

But Goncharova found it hard at first to give up her plan for the original Russian picture, (brilliantly coloured). At the same time, Larionov tried to ply me with ideas for props: a wedding-wagon, painted and decorated, some sort of 'Giant's Causeway', a long plank forming a bench which would be able to be revolved on a central axis, and so on. But in the end, when she had sat through several rehearsals, Goncharova fell in completely with my ideas.

I had imagined the costumes in a dark blue with beige blouses, whilst for her, it had to be brown, and indeed, in view of her standing as painter, it was for her to decide.

During the rehearsals, she sketched my groupings; after three days, Goncharova and Michael Larionov went back to Paris, there to continue the discussions with Diaghilev.

The costumes and décors, designed with great distinction, corresponded entirely with my choreography.

The problem of the understanding of the music did not, for me, resolve itself into strict imitation of the complicated and asymmetric rhythms of Stravinsky, by making the dance work out exactly to the internal time-signature and the notes into which it was broken down, by adapting the steps to fit them exactly; this seemed to me not only inapplicable but even absurd from the point of view of the dance.

By uniting several musical bars into a single one, I made a choreographic bar which, if it did not always match the original exactly, submitted always to the sonorities of the music. For the choreography appeared to me largely independant of the artificial divisions in the score of the work. The artists of the ballet had to resound in one single chord, like musical instruments, and to ally themselves completely with the latter.

In my own creative imagination, the choreography of *Noces* had absolutely to reflect as one whole the musical picture. Once this had been grasped, the choreographic image also created itself, genetically bound to the music and completely harmonious with it.

Whilst all this work was going on, Diaghilev showed me a lot of attention, and *Les Noces* was the only ballet for which he permitted the choreographer to have any influence whatsoever over the setting and general production.

Drawing by Natalia Goncharova for *Les Noces*, 1923

The Bronze Horseman

How a Soviet ballet is made

Natalia Roslavleva

Reprinted from Ballet Today, vol. 2, nos. 22 & 23, March, April/May 1950.
This description is true of Russian ballet in the fifties but, obviously, takes
no account of the developments since that period.

It would seem at first that *The Bronze Horseman*, the new Soviet ballet,
choreographed by Rostislav Zakharov to the music of Reinhold Glière, the
seventy-five year old dean of Russian composers, has nothing to do with con-
temporaneity. It is not so. By boldly choreographing Pushkin's immortal
poem, full of deep philosophic and dramatic significance, Soviet ballet continues the line which it has been developing throughout recent years: the
search for serious, inspiring, heroic themes, production of ballets as a complete
dramatic performance, carried out in the idiom of the dance.

The theme, however important and indicative of the trends and the tastes
in art it may be, is not a guarantee of an assured artistic success, in ballet as in
opera. Ballet demands a detailed plan of the future production, worked out by
the choreographer preferably in close contact with the composer. A good
choreographer is always author of the ballet in his own right.

Work was started on *The Bronze Horseman* as early as 1940. P. F. Abolimov,
author of the book, devoted much time to the study of material. He introduced
a three-scene prologue, in which Peter the Great was shown in meditation 'on
the bare shores' of the Neva, conceiving the future city, then 'breaking a
window into Europe', launching one of his frigates, and, lastly, entertaining at
one of his historical informal balls or 'Assemblies'.

With the exception of the first, these episodes do not actually appear in the
text of Pushkin's poem. (The only English translation of the poem, to my
knowledge, is contained in *The Poems, Prose and Plays of Alexander Pushkin*,
translated by Babette Deutsch, Random House, New York, 1936.)

The story, briefly, is of a petty official, Eugène. He loves Parasha, a simple
girl, unconnected with the splendour of Petersburg's officialdom, which he
abhors. Parasha is drowned in the flood of 1824. Eugène loses his reason. As he
roams Petersburg of the 'white nights' he challenges the Bronze Horseman –
Falconet's monument dominating the Neva embankment. It then seems to
him in his disturbed reason that the Bronze Horseman pursues him. He hears
his metallic clatter everywhere.

Russian spectators are grateful to Glière, Zakharov and Professor M. P.
Bobishov (one of his early works was the décor for Fokine's *Eros*) for reproduc-
ing one of the favourite works of Pushkin's in theatrical form. It means much,
too, that *The Bronze Horseman* is a ballet on a truly national theme. It is a
Russian work of art to its very core, for both the scenes of Peter's period and
the magnificent Petersburg of a hundred years later, the 'balagani' on the
Senate Square known to anyone who has seen *Petrushka*, the simple and
graceful Russian dances of Parasha and the girls, and the wonderful living
ensembles of the crowd. These scenes, close and dear to the Russian heart, are
gratifying in classic ballet, which has given so much space to kings, queens,

shahs, Egyptians, Spaniards, and various fantastic characters.

Abolimov read his 'book' to the Kirov theatre company on June 18th, 1941. The war broke out three days later. Composition of *The Bronze Horseman* was resumed only in 1946. Rostislav Zakharov, then just out of ballet school, started his career as choreographer in 1934 in the very same theatre with the production of *The Fountain of Bakhchiseray*, marking a very important stage in Soviet ballet. Through *The Prisoner of the Caucasus*, *Mistress into Maid*, and the opera *Ruslan and Ludmila* – his other Pushkin works – Zakharov arrived a mature master for the composition of *The Bronze Horseman*.

Having received Abolimov's brief libretto, he worked for more than a year, till the autumn of 1947, creating the detailed plan of composition for R. M. Glière. The plan consisted of forty 'numbers' with a detailed description of the contents and nature of each scene and dance and exact timing. Zakharov spent many hours in museums and libraries, studying material, archive documents, historical literature and iconography. The composition of the choreographer's plan was conducted in close contact with Glière whom Zakharov met for numerous talks.

Glière started composing the music in September 1947, and completed the score by March 1948. The orchestration, to which Glière always pays special attention, was done only by February 1949. This did not prevent the choreographer, of course, from creating the actual choreography and rehearsing the ballet.

In the course of the rehearsals it was found necessary to shorten the music. The score was reduced to the length usual for a Russian ballet – one hundred and twenty-five minutes. Glière introduced some changes into the music, naturally necessitated in the progress of the work, and altogether it may be said that the composition of the ballet lasted for a year and a half.

The music of *The Bronze Horseman* is composed according to the symphonic principle: the main themes connected with each of the pivotal characters are intensified and developed in the course of the ballet. The juxtaposition, fusion and combination of these themes make the music both deeply significant and melodious. What has not been possible to express in the actual choreography is added in the imagination by the depth of the music.

Having started the actual production of the ballet, Zakharov first of all requested from the entire company of the Kirov theatre a serious study of the period to be rendered in the ballet. This was accomplished with the help of expert advisers. It was declared, too, that there were no small parts in the ballet – all were artistically important, from Peter I to Parasha's mother.

What are the most successful scenes of the ballet? It must be said that Zakharov is above all a first-class producer, régisseur in the Russian theatrical sense of the word. Therefore he succeeded most with the wonderful scenes of purely theatrical effect, such as the flood, and the Senate Square. This only adds to Zakharov's qualities as choreographer, for in a big dramatic ballet the role of régisseur is most important and without this quality the ballet would never attain a dramatic unity.

Zakharov did create a perfectly integrated and very talented production. In the 'flood scene' which is the culminating point of the ballet, he displayed much creative imagination. With the hand of a master he arranged most impressive mises en scène and groupings. The flood starts gradually – now the crowd looks with anxiety at the water level and by the poses and expression of the people you can guess that it is rising – then the water trickles onto the embankment and the crowd starts slowly retreating before the approaching menace. At last the Neva has conquered. The stage becomes a tumult of grey and menacing waves. One can distinguish in the dim light some furniture, logs of wood, a sentry-box and even some rowing-boats carried away by the water. Eugène watches this scene from a marble lion on the flooded embankment. He had climbed its back, refusing to leave the place from which he still hoped to rescue his Parasha.

The entire scene is done in the idiom of pantomime. The effect of the flood is achieved with the help of a very simple device – the stage is covered with tarpaulin and the people moving under it in a way indicated by the choreographer create the effect of the waves. This scenic effect can hardly be compared to anything shown heretofore in ballet. It depends to a considerable extent on the lighting, but largely on the excellent rehearsing of the many people who take part in this scene and the inventive brilliancy of the producer.

Choreographically Zakharov achieved some very good results in the Russian dances of the first act and the duet of Parasha and Eugène in the second. The latter is done not as a traditional pas de deux but as a pas d'action in which the movements are justified by the meaning of the dance. Eugène performs some jumps and pirouettes because he is in love and wants to express his joy. In most of the dances Zakharov used the classical dance idiom, but he used it for a different purpose and in a different way. In the last act the corps de ballet, wearing specially designed costumes with floating draperies, faces covered with the same material, are made to convey most artistically the impression of waves, carrying away from the crazed Eugène his Parasha – the image of Parasha, whom he sees everywhere. This is a very impressive choreographic novelty, one of the most interesting from the point of pure choreography, since Zakharov has not introduced many new movements in this ballet. The vision scene in poor Parasha's little courtyard, desolate after the flood, is very touching, but when Parasha appears (as the sick imagination of Eugène sees her), one cannot help noticing several 'quotations' from *Giselle*.

There are two 'ballerina parts' in *The Bronze Horseman* – the Queen of the Ball (in the Prologue) and Parasha. They are perfectly contrasted roles. The Queen of the Ball performs a brilliant pas de deux with Peter's blackamoor servant (Pushkin's historic ancestor), whose part is danced by a good male soloist. In Moscow the role of the Queen of the Ball was taken by Marina Semyonova or Sophia Golovkina; in Leningrad, where the ballet was originally produced, by Alla Shelest.

The part of Parasha is not easy because very little is said about her not only in the 'book' but by Pushkin himself. It is merely known that she was a simple and sweet girl of a humble origin. Zakharov set some graceful and lyrical dances for Parasha mostly based on variations of the Russian dance.

In Moscow Struchkova was probably the one who succeeded best in interpreting the simple charm of Parasha. But she danced opposite Yermolayev, an unsurpassable Eugène. This ballet is in a way a male parallel of *Giselle* and it is natural that Eugène should be its central character and even overshadow the ballerina. From this point of view alone *The Bronze Horseman* is a welcome choreographic novelty, since there are practically no ballets where the male hero is the choreographic and dramatic centre. The role of Eugène shines as such, however, only in the hands of a perfect artist. Such is Yermolayev. When he dances the part of Eugène everything around him dims in the light of his artistic brilliance. He gives a touch of Dostoyevsky to his Eugène, but that is quite in the nature of the frustrated character he is impersonating. And he is not always sad and frustrated. When Yermolayev/Eugène dances his dance of young love in Parasha's little garden, he is classic in technique and at the same time most Russian and most natural. When Parasha dances her variation he settles in a nonchalant pose on the garden table and watches her with a happy smile. When he wanders, distraught, in the streets of Petersburg, pursued by a crowd of teasing boys, he is pathetic.

In Leningrad Konstantin Sergeyev created an unforgettable image of Eugène in more lyrical vein but also dominating the ballet.

The only – but unfortunate – failure of the ballet is the character of Peter the

Great in the prologue. The choreographer gave him a few static movements instead of expressive mime or dance-mime. The last scene of the ballet is also too static and amounts to a tableau vivant instead of a choreographic finale.

The motley crowd on the Senate Square in the scene where Eugène and Parasha have a rendezvous at the feet of the Bronze Horseman is beautifully done. The 'balagani' or picturesque booths are seen in the distance (the Admiralty Square where they used to be displayed adjoins that of the Senate) and some of the performers, the travelling circus and the man with the puppet theatre and street vendors fill the square. Military music sounds and a detail of hussars, preceded by dancing youths, marches across the square, admired by the strolling young ladies and their governesses. A Columbine and Harlequin are displayed by the owner of the wandering circus.

One could easily trace in this scene the inheritance of Fokine. I have been frequently asked whether it is true that the 'tradition of Imperial ballet remains unbroken in Soviet ballet' and whether in that case it has remained in the pre-Fokine era. I believe that the account of how a Soviet ballet is made, given above, is an answer to the question. However, to make the matter quite clear, I would like to recall a few historical facts.

The Fokine reform was brought about by historical necessity. The need for a reform in ballet had been felt for a couple of decades before he actually carried it out. However, great was Fokine's genius, his reform, like Noverre's, was prepared. The reform in ballet was closely interwoven with the new realistic trends in the theatre and painting. These were started not in Petersburg, but in Moscow, which was more democratic, and less conventional than imperial Petersburg. The creation of the Art Theatre in 1889 by Stanislavsky and Nemirovitch-Danchenko, the invitation by Mamontov of Korovin and Golovin as decorators for his private opera, and the first realistic production by Alexander Gorsky of *Don Quixote* in 1900 with décor by Korovin and Golovin are closely connected. Gorsky was the first to treat the corps de ballet and the whole ensemble on the stage as members of a choreographic drama, according to the principles of Stanislavsky, expecting them to act and be natural. Instead of a frozen symmetrical corps de ballet he created a living crowd; instead of the traditional accidental attire, ballet acquired for the first time real scenic costumes.

When Fokine conceived his reform in 1904 and carried it out, partly in 1906, and more fully, by 1908, he, while being considerably under the influence of the then flourishing Russian 'decadence' or art nouveau, never had the intention of breaking with the dancing tradition of the Russian ballet, with its best achievements, particularly those of the nineteenth century, or with the classic school as the only system capable of producing the perfect instrument for the choreographer to work with. He merely wanted to break the routine of the Imperial ballet, which in its worst aspects, wore corsets and diamonds, flirted and talked on the stage and had no interest in the subjects of ballets. But the best aspect of the Imperial ballet was the tradition of the Russian school – expressive dancing, inspired dancing, powerful dancing.

It would be utterly erroneous to think that Diaghilev took the Fokine reform away with him, or that in consequence of Fokine's and Diaghilev's departure 'Russian ballet remained outside the Fokine reform'. Once a reform has taken place, it cannot be stopped. Lineal choreography or flat groupings devoid of sense were abandoned for ever by Russian choreographers. But the historical truth is that Fokine created his *chef d'oeuvres*, exported by Diaghilev to the triumph of Russian art as a whole, for a special audience. Some of them, such as *Nuits d'Egypte (Cléopâtre)* were created 'pour épater la bourgeoisie'. For domestic purposes Fokine toned down his productions of the period and never allowed himself bold interpolations of music and dances from other ballets such as were done for the Paris season in order to make the ballets as striking and exotic as possible because that was what was expected from them.

Outside Russia whatever Diaghilev had in his repertoire was inherited and treated as the Gospel. But no creed should become a dogma. It should serve as a guide not as a yardstick.

It is also forgotten that Fokine broke with Diaghilev in 1912, not accidentally, but after *L'Après-midi d'un faune*, for the reason that with it Diaghilev forsook the dancing traditions Fokine never intended to give up. After 1912 Diaghilev gradually lost his 'little parliament' of invaluable collaborators and drifted eventually under the influence of French art, not Russian.

The best of the Fokine reform, what he himself was never able to achieve because he was deprived of the means, has been carried out in the Soviet ballet, an art aiming at deep significance.

What is new in Soviet ballet? Its method of realism, its function – that of reflecting true life – whether in historical or modern subjects, its preference of heroic, elevating themes, its treatment of a ballet as a fusion of all arts, directed towards an artistic whole.

The score of La Fille mal Gardée

the Royal Ballet's score by John Lanchbery and Ivor Guest

The third of three articles originally published in *Theatre Research*, vol. III, no. 3, 1961. (The first two articles dealt with the historical background of the ballet and its scores.)

In the autumn of 1959 Frederick Ashton asked John Lanchbery to produce a score for his forthcoming revival of *La Fille mal Gardée* for the Royal Ballet. A copy of the Herold score had been obtained from the Paris Opéra, the Hertel score was available in a piano reduction, and when Lanchbery had already begun his work, the original Bordeaux score was brought to light and the Fanny Elssler pas de deux discovered. Of the three main sources, the Herold score was found to be the obvious version to use for the foundation, since the Bordeaux score was altogether too archaic and over-simple, and Hertel's music too banal, hackneyed and teutonic in style. In any event, work of any length on the Bordeaux version would have proved unduly arduous since the only available material consisted of orchestral parts.

A preliminary play-through of the Herold score showed it to be a mixture of artless charm, effective borrowing and shameless padding. There were virtually no titles to the various numbers, or any other clues to link the music with the action. Furthermore, some of the music seemed quite out of place in the development of the plot, especially in Act I, and Ashton and Lanchbery spent several interesting but fruitless afternoons trying to marry the music to the story as it stood. Gradually they realized that the only solution was to write the score anew, using whatever suitable material there happened to be in context and composing the rest on some of the themes which would serve a purpose. This, then, was the method adopted, after Ashton had provided a detailed 'breakdown' of the choreographic sequences and their desired lengths (see Fig 1).

For eight weeks the two men met three times a week to discuss at length the next piece of the score to be prepared. Lanchbery would then play over what he had most recently roughed out, and this would be analysed, cut or lengthened, approved or condemned to be rewritten. In fact, the score went through the whole process of being shaped by the musician to suit the choreographer's needs. At every meeting, Ashton would make pertinent musical suggestions: 'Cut out the repeat of the second melody and give it instead an exciting sort of coda – rum-te-tum-TUM – that sort of thing,' or 'Can't the love theme come back there for a few bars?' Whole sections of the score were actually composed by Lanchbery in the style of the period, and these were most carefully vetted by the choreographer. In addition, in order to give the score the continuity and sense of purpose which were lacking in Herold's version, Lanchbery established, while trying not to work them to death, a number of themes for various characters and situations: chickens, Colas, Simone, love, butter-churning, daughter-scolding.

As soon as a section of music had been approved, Lanchbery would orchestrate it (with the copyist waiting like a hungry wolf), always bearing

1. Entrance of Simone and Lise - tired sad theme.

2. Simone busies herself with spinning wheel, then locks door and flops down.

3. Spinning diminuendo to sleep - orchestral snores. Lise tiptoes to get key but Simone wakes with a start.

4. Tambourine dance ending in Simone sleeping again, wakes again and bangs tambourine - Lise dances.

5. Simone does little dance herself (variation on clog dance).

KNOCKS AT DOOR

6. Harvesters appear and are paid.

7. Simone dresses and goes to see notary; locks Lise in.

8. Lise climbs staircase but does not see Colas - despondent - does mime scene "when I am married I will have children, three etc." - sentimental music.

Fig 1 Extract from Frederick Ashton's breakdown of the choreographic sequences: opening of Act II

the stage action very much in mind, before going on to rough out music for the next part of the scenario. While he discarded Herold's orchestration entirely* as lacking in brilliance, interest or effect, he was at the same time careful in his own work to eschew any orchestral device or texture which would appear anachronistic, with the exception of No. 28 in Act II, where in the heat of the moment he lapsed into imitation Liszt in composition as well as orchestration, and Alain's solo in Act I, where to achieve a grotesque effect, he wrote a tuba melody. Herold would not have used a tuba, but an ophicleide (in actual fact, he did not even use that), and certainly would not have written a melody for it. There is not a harp glissando in the score, and the brass writing throughout is as written in the early nineteenth century for non-valve instruments. Up-to-date percussion parts were written only where they serve a specific purpose, such as to imitate snoring, butter-churning or the clucking of chickens. For the rest, the percussion consists of the inevitable bass-drum and cymbals of the period with an occasional use of tambourine, triangle or side-drum.

The following analysis will show how the Royal Ballet score has been constructed.

* Except in Herold No. 28 ('When I am married'), where any addition to Herold's flute solo and pizzicato string accompaniment would have been superfluous.

Act I Scene I

No 1 Eleven bars of loud maestoso introduction, composed by Lanchbery, lead into Herold's opening number (Herold No 1), which is a borrowing from Martini's *Le Droit du Seigneur*. Lanchbery has slightly altered the note values of the original melody for the sake of improvement, made the harmonies rather more interesting, and written a five-bar link to:

No 2 *Dance of the Cock and Hens*. This number exists (without a title, of course) near this place in Herold's score (Herold No 3). Did they have a cock-and-hens' dance in 1828? It was the first musical point which Ashton seized on, and it is certainly most suitable music for chickens. The length of the original number has been cut by more than half, and some obvious but satisfactory bird-like counterpoint added:

Fig 2

No 3 *Lise and the Ribbon*. Here Lanchbery has joined together two of Herold's numbers with a reprise of the first (A-B-A). Both are borrowed, the first from Rossini's *Il Barbiere di Siviglia*, the second from the Bordeaux score (Herold Nos 2 and 5).

No 4 *Colas*. This, too, is taken from Herold, though only a small part has been used (Herold No 6) to be followed by a further reprise of A in No 3.

No 4a A typical 'male variation' version of No 4.

No 5 *Colas and Simone*. Nine bars of a romantic theme, composed by Lanchbery, leads suddenly into two of Herold's pieces which have been concentrated and linked together (Herold Nos 4 and 11). With the right style of scoring, they effectively depict (1) the old woman's anger and (2) her scolding tongue. The second piece becomes her theme throughout the ballet. A bridge passage has then been added which leads to:

No 6 *Villagers*. A corps de ballet number, part Herold (Herold No 10), part Lanchbery. This is linked to:

No 7 *Simone and Lise*. Again taken from Herold (Herold No 13) but tightened up. The original is for strings only: Fig 3 shows some of Lanchbery's fuller orchestration for this number.

No 8 *Lise and Colas.* A complete mélange. This important scene needed very close musical 'tailoring', as the following detailed break-down will show:

Music	Action
Five bars of Lanchbery's romantic theme, as in No 5.	Colas approaches Lise
Nine bars of the butter-churning music, first heard in No 7, dying away to	She ignores him and tries to busy herself churning butter, her actions becoming slower as she
eight bars of Martini's romantic melody from No 1, suddenly changing to	begins to listen to his pleading. He goes too far, and dares to kiss her.
four bars of churning music, dying away to	Petulantly, she returns to her butter-making but
two bars of Lanchbery's romantic theme, suddenly changing again to	pays him a moment more's attention before she decides to
four bars of churning music.	resume her task.
Two bars of the romantic theme, leading to	But when he lovingly suggests an innocent frolic, she
a new passage (Lanchbery's) of scales running up and down, and joining up with	abandons her work. They spin towards and away from one another with a ribbon, preparing for
a new polka-like number found in the Herold and Bordeaux score (Herold No 9) but here used in a shortened form with an added melody by Lanchbery which suitably leads to	A game of 'Horse and Rider'. This game gradually loses its sense of fun, as they realize that
a long statement of Martini's beautiful melody (from No 1)	love is upon them.
'Surprise' chord, and reprise of churning music.	Then, interrupted by a sudden noise, Colas hides while Lise returns to her work.

No 9 *Village girls.* A corps de ballet number based on two melodies, one by Herold (Herold No 12) and one by Lanchbery. Here, Herold's contribution has been given typical treatment: an improved melodic line and a more rhythmically and harmonically interesting accompaniment. (See Figs 4 and 5, extracts from Herold's original melody and Lanchbery's treatment of it,

Fig 3 Page 82 of Lanchbery full score (No 7)

in piano reduction form.) Half way through this number, Simone interrupts the dance, for which some of No 5 is quoted, leading straight into:

Fig 4 Extract from Herold No 12. Piano reduction

Fig 5 Extract from Lanchbery No 9. Piano reduction

No 10 *Thomas and Alain.* The elements of this number are all to be found in Herold's score. The opening pompous march theme for Thomas and the contrasting soft staccato limping phrase for his idiot son are reproduced almost note for note, and the gay dance tune which follows is a 2/4 rendering of Herold's 6/8 melody (Herold No 14). This is evidence of Ashton's determination to prune the superabundance of 6/8 in Herold's score. (See Figs 6 and 7, pages of full score of Herold and Lanchbery, showing the alteration of the melody and the more extensive scoring.) For Alain's solo, Lanchbery adapted, for ponderous tuba and occasional piccolo, a slight but appealing string melody taken from the Bordeaux score (Bordeaux No 7), which he had not wanted to discard but had hitherto been unable to place. He gave it a further allegro variation to give a final touch of brilliance to Alain's solo.

No 11 *Off to the Harvest.* A long number in rondo form, the main theme of which is Lanchbery's with quotations of previous themes, adapted to fit the 4/4 time signature, for the appearance of Colas, the chickens, etc. This number was needed to cover a difficult scene change, and could only be written when the length of time required to change the scene ($3\frac{3}{4}$ minutes) had been ascertained from the stage management.

Fig 6 Page 202 of the Herold full score (No 14)

144

146

Fig 7 Page 128 of the Lanchbery
full score (No 10), showing the
alteration of Herold's melody and the
more extensive scoring

Act I Scene II

No 12 *Colas*. A re-statement of No. 4, the Herold melody which is by now established as Colas's theme, followed by a quotation from No 11 (Off to the Harvest) but comically orchestrated to represent the cock and hens.

No 13 *Picnic*. A delicious andantino taken from the *Pas de M. Albert* (Herold No 17). Ashton required this number to accompany a humorous pas de trois for the two lovers and the idiot Alain, so Lanchbery made a number of slight alterations or musical 'points' to suit the choreographic requirements more exactly.

No 14 *Flute Dance*. After the Mozartian grace of No 13, the Flute Dance provided by Herold (Herold No 19, also found in Bordeaux score) seemed quite unsuitable, consisting as it did of a slow 6/8 air marked 'play three times'. A bright, fast-moving number for the corps de ballet was wanted instead, and Lanchbery therefore used Herold's 'Pas de Moissonneurs' (Herold No 16) with the orchestration of the opening sixteen bars strongly featuring the flute, preceded by a short linking cadenza for the same instrument.

No 15 *Quarrel*. A piece of music conceived by Lanchbery, as indeed was the situation it accompanies. Here Ashton wanted an excuse for Alain to lose his temper and stalk off in a huff, accompanied by his father and Simone, so as to remove them from the scene for the succeeding Fanny Elssler pas de deux. He suggested that Alain should seize the flute-player's instrument and try, by playing it, to lead the harvesters into an encore of No 14. Of course, he makes it sound utterly ludicrous – in the wrong tempo and the wrong key (see Fig 8) – and the corps de ballet snatch the instrument from him and goad him into the required fury.

Fig 8

No 16 *The Fanny Elssler pas de deux*. In the early days of their collaboration on *La Fille mal Gardée* Ashton and Lanchbery felt a little dejected at the poverty and unsuitability of some of Herold's music, but took great comfort at the prospect of working this pas de deux into the finished score. The origin of this pas de deux has already been told in previous articles (Vol. III, No 1, page 32 and No 2 page 131). It existed only in the form of a rough two-part rehearsal copy. Lanchbery found the orchestration of this delightful collection of airs from Donizetti operas a source of immense pleasure, and Ashton has more than matched this with superb choreography.

No 17 and 17a *Simone and her Clog Dance*. Ashton had a 'hunch' that a Clog Dance for the old mother would be a great success at this point in the ballet, and one November evening he and Lanchbery went to the Folk Dance Festival at the Royal Albert Hall for inspiration. It seemed that a moderato 12/8 Schottische-type number would be most suitable, and so, having brought on Simone with some of her music from No 5, Lanchbery concocted a Clog Dance for her in this rhythm from one of Hertel's tunes which went very well into 12/8, together with an adaptation of No 5. This was the only occasion on which a note was taken from Hertel's score. It was to be an amusing exercise to combine these Clog Dance themes of the mother with the daughter's Tambourine Dance later on, in Act II (No 23). (See Fig 9.)

No 18 *Maypole Dance*. A dance for the corps de ballet was needed here, to be interrupted at the end by the storm. After a suitable introduction of his own invention, Lanchbery constructed this number from the themes of the opening of the '*Pas de M. Albert*' (Herold No 17), adapting it so that the number of bars in each phrase fitted the rather unusual requirement of a Maypole Dance (16-16-8-16), and adding a tabor to give it a certain air of rusticity.

No 19 *Storm and Finale*. The storm from Rossini's *La Cenerentola*, which Herold had inserted (Herold No 21), has only four introductory bars before

Fig 9

148

the tempest breaks with full force. Lanchbery wrote in twelve extra bars of introduction to give a more satisfactory build-up to the splendid tutti passages. Furthermore, he had to adapt and extend the ending for the curtain effect which Ashton desired – the picture of Alain being carried rapidly heavenwards by the wind in his umbrella.

Act II

No 20 *Overture.* Herold's overture to the second act has no bearing on what has been or what is to come. Lanchbery preferred, therefore, to write his own, basing it on (a) a theme found later in Herold's second act (Herold No 30), which was to prove most useful as a 'disaster' theme when the lovers are in danger of being discovered by the mother (No 26) and (b) the andantino melody from No 13 in Act I, which was henceforth to serve as another love theme. As has already been said, it was a much easier task to fit the action to the music in Herold's second act, and Lanchbery's score for this act therefore follows the 1828 version much more closely than in any other part of the ballet. It is interesting to note that at this point three consecutive numbers are taken almost note for note from the original Bordeaux score.

No 21 *Lise and Simone.* This is based on Herold No 23. Four bars have been added to cover the rise of the curtain, and repeats of phrases have been slightly varied to avoid monotony. As in the rest of the score, the orchestration has been changed from Herold's original, which in this number is for strings only.

No 22 *Spinning.* This is made up of Herold Nos 24 and 25, with an appropriate linking passage freshly composed. Herold No 25 comes between the Spinning and the Tambourine Dance, and since the purpose behind the mother's insistence on the Tambourine Dance is to keep herself awake, it follows that in Herold No. 25, she should at least feel the danger of sleep approaching. This is a pleasant, expressive andante melody which, by being re-written at half tempo, follows naturally on the spinning music. Further the spinning motif is kept running through some of it, and a half-hearted snore is interpolated near the end with a crash chord as the mother jolts herself awake again.

No 23 *Tambourine Dance.* Following the Bordeaux score, Herold provided at this point (Herold No 26) an air with variations, dying away to a passage marked 'lent, très piano' when the mother falls asleep, which finishes half way through a bar and is followed by a resumption of the air with variations. Lanchbery's Tambourine Dance roughly follows this same pattern except that, (a) instead of lamely finishing off the *air varié* with a full close (ppp) in F major, followed by the sleeping music in the same key, he put the sleeping music into the delightfully remote key of D flat; (b) one of the love themes (No 13 and 20) is brought in during the mother's sleep to accompany a pas de deux danced by Lise, who is inside the room, and Colas, who is leaning furtively through the transom window; (c) he ended the sleep with a snore (trombone pedal-notes) and a crash chord; and (d) he combined echoes of the Clog Dance with the reprise of the Tambourine Dance (see No 17a and its musical examples).

No 24 *Harvesters.* This is based on Herold No 27, except that a soft trio passage of the original had to be made more four-square and masculine, since it was needed for male corps de ballet. Lanchbery has also done away with Herold's fortissimo ending and instead made the harvesters' melody die away as they leave the house with Simone, following this with a passage based on the second half of No 22, without the undercurrent of spinning, for Lise left on her own, to link up with*

No 25 *When I am married*. This is the same as Herold No 28, even incorporating his surprise modulation from G. major to E flat for the entrance of the melody '*La jeune et gentille Lisette*' (Herold No 29). The first part of this number is the only place where Herold's orchestration has been left untouched. Ashton wanted a strong love theme here for Colas and Lise, so Lanchbery cut the 'Lisette' air fairly short and, rather than bringing in either of the love themes so far exploited (Nos 1 and 13), restated Herold's delightful 'When I am married' melody in a richer orchestral texture.

No 26 *Simone's return*. Herold brings the 'Lisette' melody to a full close before starting his music for the mother's return. Lanchbery, on the other hand, made it interrupt the love scene at the moment of a tender kiss, and furthermore discarded Herold after the opening four bars (the 'disaster' motif with which the overture to this act begins), preferring instead to construct a musical number to fit the subsequent action more exactly, as follows:

* It is interesting to note that from the moment when the mother first falls asleep to the end of the dénouement the music of the Royal Ballet version is played without a break.

Music	Action
Four bars 'disaster' motif of Herold.	The lovers see Simone approaching through the window.
The same, extended and heightened.	Panic-stricken, they look for somewhere for Colas to hide.
A rapidly ascending passage	They run upstairs, and Colas hides in the bedroom.
dying away to a reprise of the second half of No 22 (also used when Lise was left alone in No 24).	Lise comes downstairs again, picks up a broom, and tries to look like an industrious, albeit neglected daughter.
Four bars of Simone's nagging theme (No 5 and frequently used since).	Simone bursts in,
Second half of No 22 again with	sees her daughter sweeping the floor, and
a snatch of the Clog Dance thrown in.	is pleased,
Two bars of crescendo tremolo strings.	until she notices Lise's change of kerchief. (Lise is in fact now wearing Colas's)

'Disaster' motif and its extension.	Simone berates her daughter, chases her,
The rapidly ascending passage again.	drags her upstairs, and
The nagging theme (No 5) on full orchestra,	locks her, unknowingly, in the bedroom where Colas is hiding.
interrupted by knocking music.	There is a knocking at the front door.
The nagging theme made busier, more knocking, leading to No 27.	Simone comes downstairs, busily tidies her hair, and opens the door to admit Thomas, Alain and the notary.

No 27 *Thomas, Alain and the Notary*. This at first is a restatement of No 10, except that the grotesque, rather doleful tuba solo is replaced by an equally grotesque but joyful (since Alain is expecting to marry Lise within the next ten minutes) piccolo solo based on the same melody. There follows more of his limping staccato theme, getting louder as he mounts the stairs, and leading into

No 28 *Consternation and Forgiveness*. At this vital moment of the ballet, Lanchbery found Herold so completely inadequate that he perhaps overstepped the mark and wrote in the style of Liszt rather than Herold! However, the panic-stricken nature of the music soon gives way to a timely quotation in extenso of the first love theme (No 1) to portray the overriding tenderness of the couple's love, the sad shaking of the notary's head as the marriage contract is torn up, and Simone's mother-love breaking through her shrewish nature. A loud dramatic statement in the minor of the opening theme of No 10 and No 27 with occasional notes of pathos for poor little Alain depicts the rage and headlong departure of Thomas and his son.

No 29 *Pas de deux*. A rich, full version of No 25, 'When I am married'.

No 30 *Finale*. Neither of Herold's two finales seemed particularly attractive, so Lanchbery wrote another in rondo form. He prefaced it with a few bars of No 14, for the village flute-player to raise Simone's spirits. The main rondo theme was composed by himself, but this number introduced many other themes: from Nos 6 and 18 for the villagers, from Herold's finale, from an otherwise unused melody (Herold No 20, Bordeaux No 24) for Lise, from No 4 for Colas, and from No 17a (Clog Dance) and No 23 (Tambourine Dance) for Simone. The rondo melody fades away as the dancers all skip away through the door, leaving the stage deserted until Alain, to the strains of his limping theme (Nos 10 and 27), creeps in for his umbrella, before he too scuttles out into the night.

Glossary of technical terms

This is not a manual of dance technique, but some of the technical terms may need a little explanation. Anyone wishing to delve further into the language of ballet may find excellent definitions in three books: *A French-English Dictionary of Technical Dance Terms* by Cyril W. Beaumont; *A Dictionary of Ballet Terms* by Leo Kersley and Janet Sinclair, with drawings by Peter Revitt; and the technical entries in G. B. L. Wilson's invaluable *Dictionary of Ballet* (latest edition 1974).

Arabesque   A pose in which the body is supported on one leg while the other is fully extended, with the arms disposed in harmony.

Attitude (en l'air)   A position in which the working leg is raised, usually to 90°, in front or behind the body, with the knee bent. The height of the foot in relation to the raised knee varies, depending on the school (e.g. Russian, Italian, French) in which the dancer has been trained.

Chassé assemblé   Literally a step chased and a step assembled. The foot is slid out and the weight of the body transferred to that foot, often as a jumping step and in any direction. In the assemblé the dancer brings the feet together before alighting in the required position.

Enchaînement   Literally, enchaînement, linking. A sequence of two or more steps that flow without a break into a phrase of movement. As well as being used all the time in choreography, enchaînements are devised every day in the classroom by teachers for the dancers' 'centre practice'. Choreographers, as we have indicated, often find inspiration from watching these classroom arrangements and combinations of steps.

Entrelacé   This step is either a **grand jeté en avant** or a **jeté passé** or a **grand jeté de saut** performed while turning in the air. Usually the dancer 'changes' the supporting leg while in the air, that is, if he takes off from the right foot he will land on the left foot.

Epaulement   The term used to indicate the placing of the shoulders in relation to the body. Literally, shouldering. Good épaulement can give great expressiveness to a movement or a pose. In the old Bournonville or French school there is little inclination of the shoulders and the dancers present their dance 'straight' to the audience.

Fouetté en tournant, fouetté or **temps fouetté**   A whipped movement. A difficult turning step danced on pointe in which the working leg is carried ('whipped') from the front to the side and into the **pirouette** position. This whipping movement, when co-ordinated with the use of the arms, gives the impetus for the spectacular series of turns seen in such ballets as *Swan Lake* Act III, *Les Patineurs* and others mentioned in the text. **Fouetté en tournant** is a spectacular feat for the ballerina; it is not performed by the male dancer.

Grand jeté en tournant   By derivation, a big 'thrown' step. When taken **en tournant** (turning) with a half turn, the dancer usually finishes in arabesque.

Pirouette   A full turn of the body accomplished on one leg on the full, three-quarter, half, or quarter pointe.

Retiré   The lifting of the fully turned out working thigh to right angles with the body, with the foot fully stretched and the toe placed at the very top of the calf of the supporting leg.

Revoltade   From the Italian *revoltare* (to turn over). The dancer throws the right leg up to hip level in front and then pushes off from the left leg and, taking it over the top of the right leg, lands on the left foot with the right leg in arabesque. This step is performed by the Blue Skater in his Variation in *Les Patineurs*.

Saut de basque   Turning step performed in the air with one leg straight and the other in a retiré position.

Terre à terre   Term used to indicate that the feet hardly leave the ground in the execution of a movement.

Further reading

The enormous interest in the art of ballet throughout the world today has resulted in the publication of a great many books, all of the good ones, no matter what the date of their publication, relevant in some way to the making of ballets. We give here a short and selective list. Many of the books will themselves lead on to other titles.

Balanchine, George, *Book of Ballets*, ed. Francis Mason, Doubleday, New York, 1954, reprinted as *New Complete Stories of the Great Ballets*, 1968. Stories of the ballets and with some illuminating comments from Balanchine on his own work.

Beaumont, C. W., *Complete Book of Ballets*, Putnam, London and New York, 1937, latest edition Grosset & Dunlap, New York, 1949; *Supplement to the Complete Book* 1942 and 1952; *Ballets of Today* 1954; *Ballets Past and Present* 1955. *The Complete Book* describes the work of all important choreographers (with the exception of Bournonville) from Dauberval (born 1742) to the date of publication. The other titles are in the form of Supplements. Mr Beaumont meticulously describes the action of the ballets and gives the first cast. He is particularly good on the productions he has himself seen – from 1910 onward.

Cohen, Selma Jeanne, *The Modern Dance. Seven Statements of Belief*, Wesleyan University Press, Middletown, Connecticut, 1965. The statements are by José Limón, Anna Sokolow, Erick Hawkins, Donald McKayle, Alwin Nikolais, Pauline Koner and Paul Taylor. Selma Jeanne Cohen contributes the Introduction. *Dance as a Theatre Art. Source Readings in Dance History from 1581 to the Present*, Dodd, Mead & Company, New York, 1974. Substantial translations or reprints from Fabrito Caroso (*c.* 1530–1605) to Cunningham and Nikolais today. Edited and with a commentary by Selma Jeanne Cohen.

Denby, Edwin, *Looking at the Dance*, Horizon Press, New York, 1968; *Dancers, Buildings and People in the Streets*, Horizon Press, New York, 1965. Brilliant criticism by just about the best writer on ballet.

De Valois, Ninette, *Invitation to the Ballet*, John Lane, London 1937 and Oxford University Press, New York, 1938. *Come Dance with Me*, Hamish Hamilton, London, 1957 and World, New York, 1958. The founder of Britain's Royal Ballet sets out in the first book her beliefs about the function of a repertory company. The second book is a more personal memoir.

Graham, Martha, *Notebooks*, Harcourt Brace Jovanovich, New York, 1973. Discusses her work since the 1940s.

Kirstein Lincoln, *Movement and Metaphor*, Sir Isaac Pitman & Sons Ltd, London, 1970. A superb analysis of the component parts of ballet is followed by a history of the art traced through fifty seminal works. Magnificent illustrations. *The Book of the Dance*, Putnam, New York, 1935 and Dance Horizons, New York, 1969. A history that traces the art of dancing from myth, ritual and the Greek theatre to the date of publication. *The New York City Ballet*, Knopf, New York, 1973. The lavish presentation should not conceal a valuable text. Very many illustrations which give a particularly good idea of the choreography of George Balanchine.

Percival, John, *Experimental Dance*, Studio Vista, London and Universe, New York, 1971. Containing a number of pertinent observations from contemporary choreographers.

Taper, Bernard, *Balanchine*, Harper & Row, New York, 1963 and Collins, London, 1964. The definitive biography of the choreographer.

History

Brinson, Peter and Crisp, Clement, *Ballet for All*, Pan, London, 1970 and David & Charles, Newton Abbot, Devon, 1971. Describes most of the ballets in the repertory today. Very good on the nineteenth-century ones which have survived.

Clarke, Mary and Crisp, Clement, *Ballet. An Illustrated History*, A & C Black, London and Universe, New York, 1973. Traces the development of the art from the Renaissance courts today. A lively text, informative captions and no fewer than 253 illustrations. Reading lists at the end of each chapter.

Guest, Ivor, *The Dancer's Heritage*, Dancing Times, London, 1960. An excellent concise history. The recommended textbook for G.C.E. 'O' Level Ballet.

Lawson, Joan, *A History of Ballet and its Makers*, Dance Books, London, 1964. Traces the development through the work of choreographers and ballet masters.

Soviet Ballet

Roslavleva, Natalia, *Era of the Russian Ballet*, Gollancz, London, 1966. The 'official' story of ballet in Russia.

Swift, Mary Grace, *The Art of the Dance in the USSR*, University of Notre Dame Press, Indiana and London, 1968. An impartial survey of how ballet survived the Revolution and has developed since under the Soviet régime.

Music

Searle, Humphrey, *Ballet Music*, revised ed. Dover, New York, 1973. The best available introduction to the subject.

Shead, Richard, *Constant Lambert*, Simon Publications, London, 1973. Lambert was musical adviser to and principal conductor of Britain's Royal Ballet in its formative years.

Design

Beaumont, C W, *Ballet Design Past and Present*, Studio Publishing, London, and Studio, New York, 1947. A panorama of settings and costumes over the centuries.

Buckle, Richard, *Modern Ballet Design*, A & C Black, London, 1955. Deals with the designers who contributed most in the immediate post-World War II years, including the brilliant French.

Reade, Brian, *Ballet Designs and Illustrations, 1581–1940*, HMSO, London, 1967. The collection in the Victoria and Albert Museum.

Rowell, Kenneth, *Stage Design*, Studio Vista, London, and Van Nostrand Reinhold, New York, 1968. An excellent introduction with much material about ballet design.

Technique

Beaumont, C W and Idzikowski, Stanislas, *A Manual of Classical Theatrical Dancing*, C Beaumont, London, 1922. The precepts of Maestro Enrico Cecchetti.

Bruhn, Erik and Moore, Lillian, *Bournonville and Ballet Technique*, A & C Black, London, 1961. The 'Danish School' explained.

Stuart, Muriel and Kirstein, Lincoln, *Classic Ballet*, Knopf, New York, 1952 and Longmans, London, 1953. The precepts of the School of American Ballet.

Vaganova, Agrippina, *Basic Principles of Classical Ballet*, A & C Black, London, 1948 and Dover Publications, New York, 1969. The system on which all Soviet teaching is now founded.

Periodicals

In Britain: *The Dancing Times, Dance and Dancers* – illustrated monthlies that, in addition to news and reviews, frequently contain interviews with ballet makers.

In the US: *Dance Perspectives* – scholarly quarterly paperbacks, rich in illustrations; *Ballet Review* – an 'occasional' journal, lively writing, and many contributions from dancers and choreographers.

Index

Sources of illustrations

Page 21 photograph by Gordon Anthony; page 33 *bottom*, 35, 38, 40, 48, 51, 64–5, 76, 99 by Anthony Crickmay; pages 39, 41, 44, 46 by Alan Cunliffe; page 17 from the Dance Collection of the New York Public Library; page 27 *bottom* by J. W. Debenham; pages 56, 100 by Zoë Dominic; page 31 by Fred Fehl; page 50 by Foto somo; page 24 by Philippe Halsman, page 11 *top* by van Haven; page 107 by François Hers/Viva; pages 68, 89, 91 by Houston Rogers; page 11 *bottom* by John R. Johnson; page 34 by Peggy Leder; page 28, 93 by Denis de Marney; page 37 by Jack Mitchell; page 52 by Mydskov; page 92 *top* by Oleaga; page 90 *bottom* by Stuart Robinson; page 36 by Roy Round; page 86 by Frank Sharman; page 88 by Donald Southern; page 57 by Leslie E. Spatt; page 29 by Martin Swope; pages 83, 84, 85 from the Victoria and Albert Museum, London; page 27 *top* by Victor Welch; page 33 *top* by Wilfoto; page 30 by G. B. L. Wilson; page 90 *top* by Reg Wilson.